Praise for Donna
and *Orphan Train To Kansas*

"An honor to share the stage with you!"

—Christina Baker Kline
New York Times bestselling author of the novel, *Orphan Train*

"A wonderful depiction of American life in the early days of the twentieth century, sure to educate and entertain readers of all ages."

—Dianne K. Salerni, Author of *The Eighth Day* Series – Harper Collins

"Filled with action, the reader is lucky enough to hop on the train right alongside Oliver!"

—Jessica Strawser, Editor – *Writers Digest*

"A moving story of the determination of children, sure to please."

—James A. Cox, Editor-in-Chief – *The Midwest Book Review*

"An important part of American history written in an engaging and readable style. Understanding the settlement of the Plains from a personal perspective is a powerful method for teaching history."

—Peter N. Jones, PhD – Cultural Anthropologist

"Excellent book! This story touches on brotherly love and the importance of family, in addition to the historical contribution."

—Renee Wendinger, Minnesota Orphan Train Assoc.
Author of *Extra! Extra! The Orphan Trains & Newsboys of New York*

Dear Sue —
We hope that you enjoy
these books + DVD! Love,
Beth + Mark

ORPHAN TRAIN
TO KANSAS

A True Story

DONNA NORDMARK AVILES

Wasteland Press

www.wastelandpress.net
Shelbyville, KY USA

Orphan Train to Kansas
by Donna Nordmark Aviles

First Printing – January 2018
ISBN: 978-1-68111-219-0

Printed in the U.S.A.

0   1   2   3   4   5   6   7   8

For my father, Benjamin Nordmark, who took the time to share the stories of Oliver's childhood. I thank him for leading by example.

Dedicated in honor and memory of the children who rode America's orphan trains – especially Oliver and Edward. May their stories never be forgotten, and may we learn from them the value of every child.

"When a child of the streets stands before you in rags, with a tear-stained face, you cannot easily forget him. And yet, you are perplexed what to do. The human soul is difficult to interfere with. You hesitate how far you should go."
—Reverend Charles Loring Brace

I extend my deepest appreciation to author, historian, and orphan train descendant, Clark Kidder of Janesville, Wisconsin. His tireless research unearthed the photograph on the cover of this book depicting a "Company Sent West, March 31, 1908." This photograph includes my grandfather, Oliver Nordmark, along with his brother, Edward. This is the earliest photograph of Oliver and the *only* photograph known to exist of Edward. I am so very grateful. Thank you, Clark.

INTRODUCTION

In 1853, Reverend Charles Loring Brace established the Children's Aid Society, in an effort to help the estimated 30,000 homeless and neglected children living on the streets of New York City. Between 1854 and 1929, the Children's Aid Society, along with the New York Foundling Home and other smaller organizations, relocated an estimated 250,000 children. The children left New York City, initially traveling to farming communities of the Midwest. By 1929 however, every state within the continental United States had received at least one child. It was believed that the farmers would welcome the children and take them into their families. In return, the children would supply much needed help with the labors of farm life. Later known as The Orphan Train Movement, this was the forerunner of today's Foster Care system.

This book is the true story of my grandfather, Oliver Nordmark, and his younger brother, Edward. Together they rode one of America's orphan trains from New York City to Kansas in 1908. Oliver was just nine years old and Edward was six. Their story is one of perseverance, resilience and love.

As a grown man, Oliver lived by the lessons learned by many orphan train riders – "nothing ventured, nothing gained" ... "no one is looking out for you, except you"... and finally, "bad things will happen, but it's up to you to decide if you let those bad things define you, or if you choose to put them behind you and go forward." Oliver chose the latter. He was thankful to Reverend Brace and the Children's Aid Society for giving him a chance at a better life. He made the most of it!

—Donna Nordmark Aviles

CHAPTER ONE
Oliver's Hooky Day

Oliver sat upright as he gazed out of the open window, soaking in all the colors of early spring. As the passenger train chugged along on its journey westward, he rocked gently back and forth to the rhythm of the squeaking rails. Any passerby along the tracks might presume that the young boy had not a care in the world. Oliver looked at the situation he presently found himself in, as the start of a big adventure – maybe the biggest adventure of his life! Watching the scenery unfold before him, he saw sights he never even knew existed. Having never left New York City in all his nine years, he was amazed at the openness and gently rolling hills of the grasslands before him. They seemed to Oliver to extend as far as the eye could see. He wondered if the place where the blue sky met the tall grass was the beginning of Heaven. If he could walk to that place, would he be able to see his mum again? It seemed so peaceful there... would she be smiling?

Every now and then, the train slowed to a near crawl as it passed through small villages etched out of the dust and grass. Each village had a weather-beaten wooden platform next to the tracks, but only once so far had Oliver seen people waiting to board a train. His train never stopped at the platforms, so he began to think that somehow this was a special train, carrying special children. He counted himself and his brother Edward, three years his junior, among those special people. Oliver glanced at Edward as he slept soundly, his head leaning on Oliver's arm. Instinctively, he knew that he was now his brother's keeper.

Oliver – Back Row, 3rd From Right... Edward – Front Row, 4th From Right

As he sat and took it all in, breathing deeply of the fragrant air, he couldn't help but think of his tenth birthday, just six months away. Although he hadn't a clue as to where he was headed, he did know where he had been. Almost two years ago, Oliver had turned eight years old on October 8, 1906. His teacher, Mrs. Petty – or Mrs. *Pretty* as Oliver secretly called her – had brought a small chocolate cake to school and placed it on the desk right in front of him. She led the class in "Happy

Birthday To You" and asked him if he would like to share his cake with the other students.

"No, no, a hundred times no," thought Oliver. Aloud, however, he said, "If you think I should, Mrs. Pret... ah... Petty."

Oliver's heart sank in his chest as he watched Mrs. Petty take his cake to her desk and carefully slice it into small pieces – one for each of his classmates. As his hand brought the first bite to his lips, Oliver thought it must be the most delicious confection he had ever tasted. He savored every crumb, all the time thinking that Mrs. Petty must really think he was something special to bake him a cake. His own mother had never done that.

Thinking about that happy day, Oliver's thoughts drifted back to his home – the only real home he had ever had. *405 East 19th Street, New York City.* His mother, Elizabeth – or Lizzie as everyone called her – had made him memorize his address for as long as he could remember.

"Just in case you get lost, Oliver. You can tell any shopkeeper and they will help you find your way," she used to say.

Of course, Oliver knew he would never get lost. He knew his neighborhood like the back of his hand. He even knew how to get to Madison Avenue and back. Oliver's father, Otto, was a tailor by trade. He worked in the main room of the family's two room apartment. His big tailor's table took up most of the room. Handmade racks, that his father had built, held the finished work of his trade. Those racks were used to transport his father's suits to the fancy shops of Madison Avenue. Otto had trusted his oldest son, at the young age of eight, to push those racks all the way to Madison. Oliver felt proud and very grown up to be delivering his father's suits – very fine suits indeed, he was sure of that.

Oliver tried to think back to those times... when had things begun to change? Several months after that happy day at school on his eighth birthday, Oliver had overheard some of the bigger boys in the schoolyard talking about playing "hooky" from school. Having never even heard of hooky, Oliver had listened intently as they joked about all the fun they had and how they were going to do it again. From what he could gather, it seemed to Oliver that hooky was something every kid should try. It was like a holiday from school, except the kid got to decide when the holiday would be. He wondered why Mrs. Petty hadn't mentioned this to the class. Maybe she had explained it when he was home sick with that terrible fever at the start of school. Yes, that must be it. She just forgot that Oliver had not been there when she explained it. Well, he certainly did not want to point out to his pretty young teacher that she had made a mistake. So on his own, Oliver decided when his "hooky day" would be. Tomorrow, of course! Tomorrow would be a perfect day for hooky!

The next morning was sunny and cool. Oliver woke early, filled with excitement about his hooky day. He quickly dressed in his knickers and sweater, pulled on his cap and grabbed a few spoonfuls of oatmeal that his mother had set out for him.

As he ran down the steps of the apartment building, his mother called out from the open door, "Oliver, don't forget your Reader!"

"I don't need it today!" he shouted back over his shoulder. He could hear continued protests from his mother, but he didn't stop to explain. This was one day he didn't want to be late!

Arriving at the schoolyard, Oliver waited for the ringing of the bell, which signaled the start of the school day. He watched as his schoolmates filed into the building, their book straps over their shoulders and tin lunch buckets in their hands.

With a bounce in his step and a whistle on his lips, the happy second grader frolicked up and down the block in front of his school. His own hooky day! What fun indeed! Oliver skipped a stone, kicked a dirty old bottle, and was thoroughly enjoying his day of freedom. Not long after he had begun his holiday, Oliver heard a shout from a second story school window.

"Hey, what are you doing?" a boy called out to Oliver.

Grinning from ear to ear, Oliver replied, "Having my hooky day. It's great!"

Later that day, as the school children filed out to the yard to eat from their lunch pails, Oliver heard his name.

"Oliver Nordmark!" called out Mrs. Petty. "What in the world are you up to?"

Looking only slightly confused, Oliver responded, "I'm having my hooky day!" Mrs. Petty's face turned red in anger. Now he was *really* confused.

"Get in here right this instant!" she screamed at him.

Not knowing what to do, and not liking the look on his teacher's face, Oliver decided he'd better listen. He walked onto the schoolyard with his head down. Mrs. Petty grabbed him by the ear and pulled him into the building.

Marching him into the classroom, she shouted to Oliver, "Hold out your hands!"

With a quivering lip, Oliver slowly raised his arms, hands extended. Before he could make any sense of what was happening, Mrs. Petty reached for her yardstick and cracked him on the knuckles just as hard as she could. *Crack! Crack! Crack!* Wincing in pain, Oliver tried hard to hold back every tear.

CHAPTER TWO

Oliver Goes

to Prison

"You know," Oliver now thought, as he looked out over the passing prairie, "I think that was the ruination of me, right then and there. Hooky day, my eye! Yes, I do believe that was the start of *all* this."

He was right of course. The very next day at school, Oliver was called out of his class to the Headmaster's office. As he entered, he noticed a tall man in a rumpled suit with thin stripes. The man's shoes were scuffed and he carried a brown case that looked, to Oliver, like a small suitcase.

The man looked Oliver square in the eye and spoke firmly, "Delinquency will not be tolerated in our schools, young man. You will be coming with me for a period of detention, in an effort to correct your behavior."

Oliver gave the man a puzzled look but decided he had better do as he was told to avoid any further trouble. Silently, he followed the man out of the building.

* * * *

Edward stirred in the seat, momentarily breaking Oliver's train of thought. "I'm hungry," Edward whispered, as he looked up through glassy eyes.

"There's nothing to eat yet," replied Oliver. As he looked down at Edward's small, sad face, Oliver reached into his pocket and took out half a gingersnap. "Here," he said as he handed the treat to Edward, "This is the last I have."

Edward promptly sat up straight to enjoy his treat as Oliver's arm reached around his brother's shoulder. Somewhere in his mind, Oliver knew that giving Edward his last gingersnap was only the beginning of the many sacrifices ahead. After all, who else did Edward have now? He was only a boy of six. Who would look out for him if not Oliver?

* * * *

Having calmed Edward with the gingersnap, Oliver's mind wandered back to the tall man in the suit. Oliver had ridden that day in the man's horse-drawn buggy, through the streets of New York City, to a tall skyscraper building. Above the front door were the words GUARISH SOCIETY. He wondered what that might mean. He was taken to a room on the ninth floor. He remembered that because he had counted, at the top of each staircase, all the doors that they *didn't* enter. At the ninth door, the man took a large key from his pocket. He opened the door, then led Oliver to a room on the left side of the dimly lit hallway. It was a small room with one window. There were six small metal beds with old straw mattresses. There were no sheets and no pillows. Oliver looked around for blankets but found none. In fact, there was nothing else in the room. To Oliver, it looked like a prison. Although he had never seen a prison, he was sure that this must be what one would look like. Without a word, the man left the room. He closed and locked the door behind him. *Bang! Clang!*

"Yep," thought Oliver, "I'm in prison."

Oliver walked slowly around the dirty room looking into every nook and cranny. There were many kinds of bugs scurrying in the corners. That didn't bother him much. Oliver had seen so many bugs in his apartment building that he didn't think much about them... just a part of life. He climbed up on the furthest bed and looked out through the bars of the small window.

"Wow," Oliver heard himself say out loud to no one, "I can see all of New York City from here!"

What a great distraction. Oliver quickly forgot all about his troubles and reached his neck as far as he could to see as much as possible. Looking straight down, he saw something quite odd. There below him in a vacant lot, was something moving around in circles. But what was it? It looked like little monkeys moving around on three wheels. There was one big wheel in the front and two smaller wheels in the back. The monkeys were holding on to something but Oliver couldn't quite make out just what it was. He stood at the edge of the bed on his tip toes watching the monkeys for what seemed like a long time. Suddenly, the door to his prison opened up and three boys came in. The door slammed behind them.

Oliver was pretty sure that these boys were older than he was, but he managed a slight grin and said, "Hi, I'm Oliver."

"Well, get down off my bed, Oliver, and don't go near it again! I'm George and I'm in charge in *this* room. Now don't you forget it!"

"I'm sorry," Oliver replied. "I was just watchin' them monkeys down in that lot goin' round and round."

George looked sideways at Oliver then walked over and looked out the window. "Monkeys?" He looked at Oliver with distain. "What are you, stupid or somethin'? Those ain't no monkeys. That's boys on bicycles. Boys who are *not* in trouble like you are. Now sit on your own bed and shut up."

Oliver did as he was told and sat down quietly on the bed furthest from George's. He thought about what George had said – boys riding bicycles. Oliver had never seen a bicycle in his life. Boys rode them. Hmmm... "I'm going to have a bicycle someday," he thought. The fun of watching the monkeys, as he had imagined they were, was over – over for good. This was prison, and there would be no fun with monkeys – imagined or real.

* * * *

Oliver remembered staying in the prison for about a week. He was fed two meals each day. The first meal was a runny oatmeal that tasted very bland. His mother had always added a little sugar, but there was no sugar in prison. Later in the day, the boys were fed soup broth that had things floating in it. His mother had sometimes put a ham bone and vegetables in the soup she made. There was no ham, or meat of any kind, in prison. Oliver hoped that it might be bits of vegetables that he dodged with his spoon, but just to be sure, he never ate anything he didn't recognize as edible. Sometimes there was a hard crust of bread that came with the broth. Oliver would dip this in his bowl to make it a little softer before eating it. At home, he would spread a small pat of vegetable oil or hardened butter onto his bread. Bread, if served at all, was served stale and plain in prison, but Oliver ate it anyway. His hungry stomach wouldn't let him pass it up.

CHAPTER THREE
Orphanage Bound

A s the week passed, there was no change in Oliver's daily prison
routine. Most of his time was spent either sleeping, sitting on his bed
daydreaming, or eating his meager meals. Twice each day, the guard came
and took the boys down the metal stairs and outside to a small fenced lot
where they were led in basic exercises. Oliver was happy to at least be out
in the fresh air. He followed along with the exercises as best he could,
wondering just how long he was going to be in jail... until he was
twelve?... until he was grown-up?... until he died? His answer came that
Saturday morning.

Just as Oliver was getting ready to follow the other boys to the big
room for his breakfast, the door to the room slammed open. Oliver was
truly giddy by the sight before him. He saw an older woman in a long gray
dress with a white apron. A gray and white cap rested in her hair. She
stood behind a man in a striped suit. It was the same man who had called
Oliver out of Mrs. Petty's classroom and brought him to prison. Neither

the man nor the woman, however, was the reason for Oliver's glee. It was the small boy, hiding behind the woman's skirt, that spread a smile so wide across Oliver's face that he thought he might burst. Edward, his little brother just five years old, peeked at Oliver, his dimpled cheeks smiling.

"Edward! My brother Edward!" Oliver shouted excitedly. He ran to hug Edward, who instinctively reached out for him.

The woman never spoke as she watched the boys embrace. A quick thought passed through Oliver's mind. They couldn't be putting Edward in jail too, could they? He was much too little to be here. No, no, something else must be going on. So many thoughts were running through Oliver's mind that he couldn't settle on just one. Very abruptly, the tall man supplied the answer.

"Come with us now, Oliver. I'm afraid your mother has died and your father is ill and cannot care for you. Mrs. Thompson and I will be escorting both of you to the The Children's Village Orphanage. That's where you'll be living from now on."

"What about my big sister, Anna?" Oliver managed to quietly ask, trying to digest the meaning of the man's simply stated facts.

"Anna has been transferred to the Catholic Protectory for Girls in the Bronx section of New York City," he said.

"Well," thought Oliver, "I hope orphanages are better than jails." So many thoughts rushed around in his head... his mother had died... how had that happened?... was that why no one had come for him in prison?... at least he had Edward... his father was sick?... would his father be able to find them in the orphanage when he got better?... would he die too?... what would happen to him and Edward?

* * * *

Oliver peered out the window of the carriage as he traveled with Edward through the streets of New York City. He wasn't near his neighborhood, so Oliver really had no idea how far they had gone or in what direction they were headed. Edward nodded off to sleep as he rested his head against Oliver's arm. After nearly a week in prison, it felt good to have his little brother so close. As the carriage pulled into a long drive, Oliver's stomach began to growl and he realized that he had not eaten yet.

"We're here," stated Mrs. Thompson.

Oliver wriggled in his seat trying to make himself taller to see what was before them. His wriggling stirred Edward, who rubbed his eyes and hung onto Oliver's arm.

"Mum... where's Mum?" Edward mumbled sleepily.

Looking down at his younger brother, Oliver decided not to answer. He couldn't make sense of any of this himself. How could he be expected to explain it to Edward?

The carriage door opened and as Oliver stepped out, Mrs. Thompson helped Edward out and headed toward the door of the orphanage. Oliver fell in behind as they entered the main hall. Once inside, they were greeted by an older woman. She took Edward's hand from Mrs. Thompson.

"Well, you just come with me little fellow. I'll get you some nice warm clothes and a hot lunch. How does that sound?" she cooed to Edward.

"What about me?" Oliver spoke just above a whisper. "I'm hungry too."

"You'll be going with Matron O'Brien to the school age cottages," replied the older woman. "She'll be along shortly."

As Edward and the older woman disappeared down the long hall, Oliver had no idea that it would be nearly a year before he would see the sweet face and dimpled cheeks of his little brother again. Sitting down on a long wooden bench in the hallway, Oliver began idly counting the graying tiles of the floor.

"Come along now, Oliver," called Mrs. Thompson. Her sudden, sharp voice startled Oliver from his daydreaming. She had been in a nearby office, along with the man in the striped suit. A large woman in a uniform was with her. Oliver figured that this must be Matron O'Brien. The four of them exited through the big front door and down the stone steps. Mrs. Thompson and the tall man reached for the carriage door handles, but only Mrs. Thompson glanced back to look at him.

"Good-bye, Oliver. Good luck." She climbed into the carriage and rode away.

Oliver turned to look at Matron O'Brien. He was momentarily startled to see that she had already started walking down the path alongside the big building. He quickly ran to catch up with her. Walking along the path, Oliver was distracted by all that he saw around him. There were houses, like cottages, situated along the path. Some sat right near the path while others were further back on paths of their own. There were tall trees, many in full bloom. Matron O'Brien took a sudden turn onto a side path and quickly reached the door of Butler Cottage.

Finally, she spoke. "Now this is your new home Oliver – Butler Cottage."

They crossed the threshold and entered the front room. Oliver took a quick glance around, noticing a long table with lots of straight chairs along the back wall. He also saw a large fireplace with logs neatly stacked to one side. There were smaller tables and chairs in the front part of the room with books in the center of each table. Colorful curtains hung from the windows and woven rugs covered large areas of the wooden floor boards. Along the left side of the room, just inside the front door, Oliver saw a row of large hooks. Dark blue coats hung from nearly every hook and there were boots on the floor under each coat. Everything seemed very clean to Oliver, having just spent the better part of a week in a bug infested jail.

Boys Cottage at The Children's Village Orphanage, Dobbs Ferry, NY

"Now this is our cottage main room," began Matron O'Brien. "This is where you and your housemates do your lessons. We have meals there on the back table – breakfast, lunch and dinner. If you are late for meals you do not eat. Is that understood?"

"Yes, Matron O'Brien. I won't be late," Oliver quickly replied.

"Your sleeping quarters are upstairs. Follow me," continued Matron O'Brien.

Oliver climbed the curved staircase staying close on Matron O'Brien's heels. Reaching the top stair, Oliver looked around and was very pleased by what he saw. Unlike the jail he had just left, there were no straw mattresses devoid of bedding and pillows. No, this was just the opposite. On each wall he saw five beds. Each bed was painted white and had a real mattress. The mattresses were covered with blue blankets and pillows in white cases. Next to each bed was a white metal cabinet, tall and narrow. There were windows on each side of the room with blue and white checked curtains pulled back to let in the light of the day. A large oval shaped, braided rug warmed the wooden floor boards in the center of the room. Matron O'Brien led Oliver to the far bed on the right side of the room.

"This will be your bed and clothes locker. You are responsible for keeping this bed perfectly made without a wrinkle, just the way you see it now." Swinging the door of the cabinet open, she continued, "These are your uniforms. There are two shirts, two knickers, and one set of bed clothes. You are to wear each shirt and knickers for three days. On the fourth day you are to place your dirty uniform in the laundry cart over there." She pointed to the left of the staircase where, indeed, there stood a white cart. "By the time you wear your second uniform for three days, your first uniform will be back clean from the laundry." Matron O'Brien headed for the stairs. Calling over her shoulder, she further instructed Oliver, "Now change into your uniform and meet me downstairs. Your housemates will be returning from their morning chores shortly, and we will be preparing our noon meal." With that, she disappeared down the stairs.

Oliver looked around. He opened his cabinet and looked inside. Everything was there, even a pair of brown shoes. He gently slid his fingertips across the neatly made, wrinkle-free bed. Picking up the small pillow, he brought it to his chest and buried his little boy's face into the cushion of feathers. Tears slowly spilled from Oliver's eyes into the soft white case. The gravity of his situation began to sink in. He was in a strange place, with strange people, strange rules and no idea what to do next. His thoughts turned to Edward. Did Edward have a bed to make each morning, free of wrinkles? Oliver was fairly certain that Edward would not even know what wrinkles were, let alone how to make them go away.

"Oh Mum," Oliver's quivering lips whispered through his tears, "I'm scared, Mum."

CHAPTER FOUR
Life at the Orphanage

Oliver's short-lived joy at seeing his young brother, Edward, was quickly replaced with a sad longing for all he had lost. Life in the orphanage cottage under the supervision of Matron O'Brien was very strict and constantly supervised. Each morning the boys would rise at 6:00 AM to the sound of a loud bell. They went to the washroom where bowls of room temperature water sat lined up on a long table. Each boy quickly washed up with a coarse, scent-free soap. They scrubbed their teeth with baking soda, then scurried back to their room to replace their nightshirts with uniforms. At the sound of the second bell, all ten boys lined up at attention across the front of their room. Matron O'Brien would pass along the line with a long pointer in her hand. She looked every boy up and down, inspecting uniforms, checking for clean hands and faces, and making sure everyone's hair had been combed into place. After the inspection, the boys filed down the stairs to the breakfast table.

Here's a whole cottage family out for a ride

Meal times passed in silence, no talking was allowed. Whatever food arrived on the plate in front of the boys, they were required to eat it with no questions asked. And eat it they did! The boys were kept so busy and worked so hard at chores that they were always hungry. Second helpings of food did not exist. When the meal was finished, it was finished. Oliver really didn't mind the taste of most of the meals served in Butler Cottage. His mother had never been an elaborate cook, mostly because there was not a lot of money to cook anything fancy. Her meals were tasty and filling, just not fancy. If something was served at the orphanage that he truly did not like, Oliver would close his eyes and imagine his mother's oatmeal with sugar, or her stew with turnips, and pretend that the meal in front of him tasted as good.

Months passed and before Oliver knew it, winter had arrived. Snow covered the grounds of the orphanage and the boys were kept busy with shoveling snow, cutting wood, and gathering enough kindling to keep their cottage warm. Fires were kept burning in the main room's fireplace during the day. At night, however, the fire went out and the boys were often quite chilly as they tried to sleep in the second floor bedroom.

* * * *

As Oliver rode along on the train headed west, the long, low calling of the steam engine's whistle rang through his head. It quickly reminded him of another whistle that sounded that cold winter at the orphanage. The first time he had heard it, Oliver quickly turned to his housemate William, who was helping him shovel the front walk.

"What's that whistle for?" Oliver asked, with his eyebrows raised in fear.

"That's the whistle from the powerhouse," William replied. "They got a jail inside the powerhouse, and they sound the whistle every time someone gets sent to the jail for breaking a rule."

Oliver looked over at William. "Any rule?"

"*Any* rule," was William's reply of warning.

Oliver finished his shoveling, knowing full well that he would not be breaking any rules. Having already been to jail, he was going to make sure that he never ended up there again.

Oh, if only he had known! The very next morning, Oliver and his housemates woke to the 6:00 AM bell. As he rubbed his sleepy eyes to see the light of day, Oliver noticed that he not only saw light, he could also see his breath! It had gotten so cold during the night that Oliver's skin was covered with goose bumps and his ears were ice cold. Returning from the washroom, Oliver had what he thought was a brilliant idea. Since his clean uniform had come back from the laundry just the evening before, and he still had one more day left to wear his current uniform before it had to go in the laundry, Oliver decided to put both his shirts on to try and fend off the cold. Standing nice and tall in the inspection line, Oliver held back a grin of pride at having been so clever. As Matron O'Brien passed in front of him, she stopped abruptly.

"Oliver Nordmark! What do you think you're doing?" She pulled Oliver by the arm over to his bed. "Remove that shirt!" she barked at him. Oliver unbuttoned his shirt, revealing the second shirt underneath. "You have broken the uniform rules young man. It's the powerhouse for you!"

Matron O'Brien took Oliver by the arm and escorted him all the way to the powerhouse. As she pushed him through the door, she stated firmly, "Rules are made to be followed, Oliver. The sooner you accept that in life, the better off you'll be."

The heavy door slammed behind him, and the powerhouse whistle sounded for the arrival of another captive orphan.

CHAPTER FIVE
The Powerhouse Jail

Turning from the slammed door, Oliver looked into the jail and was surprised by what he saw. There were several windows on each wall that were covered with thick, black iron bars in a crisscross pattern. There was a big ring painted on the floor of the open room. Oliver did not see any cell doors around the room. Boys of all ages milled about inside the ring. Men in uniforms with big sticks stood around the outside of the ring. Before he could even open his mouth to speak, one of the guards took him by the elbow and shoved him into the ring.

"Stay inside the ring unless you wanta get beat!" the guard shouted. Oliver walked quickly and quietly to the center of the ring, trying not to be noticed. He fought back a tear and tried to look brave.

"Don't pay no 'tention to him," a tall boy of about twelve said to Oliver. "He ain't never beat no one yet, far as I can tell."

Breathing a short sigh of relief, Oliver looked around for a familiar face. Sadly, he found none. Within a few minutes, there were loud banging and clanging noises and all the boys dropped down to a sitting position. Oliver quickly did the same, not wishing to stand out. Big metal carts were being pushed to the edge of the circle where the guards grabbed the trays from inside and hurriedly passed them among the seated boys.

"Ah, breakfast!" Oliver thought. He quickly devoured the lukewarm mush. It was runny and tasteless but filled his small stomach nonetheless. A guard's stick banging against the metal cart signaled the end of breakfast, and all the boys slid their trays to the edge of the circle. The guard swatted his stick on the shoulders of two boys sitting near the circle's edge. They leapt to their feet and began scurrying around the circle, picking up and stacking the trays back into the cart. When the task was complete, they quickly returned to the ring.

Around mid-morning, a shrill bell sounded and all the boys got down on their backs in straight lines. Again, Oliver moved as quickly as possible to find a line with room for him, so as not to stand out. Within seconds, a guard began pacing back and forth along one side of the ring shouting out different exercises for the boys to do.

"Sit ups!" he bellowed. "One, Two, Three, Four, One, Two, Three, Four!"

Oliver tried to keep up with the other boys. He was sure he skipped one every now and then but hoped that the guard wouldn't notice.

"On your stomachs!" was the guard's next command. "Push-ups!" he shouted over their heads. "One, Two, Three, Four, One, Two, Three, Four!"

This went on for so long that Oliver thought he would collapse from exhaustion. He hung in there as best he could and counted his blessings that he was not singled out for cheating when he got behind on the count. Finally, the bell sounded again and all the boys stood up and began mingling about.

After a lunch which followed the same routine as breakfast, the guards began escorting the boys in groups of four to the bathroom. There were no doors to the bathroom and Oliver was embarrassed to find that the guard stood watch over them the whole time. With his head down, he quickly went about his business and returned to the ring. He was certain that his face was as red as a beet!

As the day wore on and night approached, the guards pushed woven mats into the ring. The boys each grabbed a mat and spread them out on the floor. Curling up on his mat, Oliver briefly thought about asking for a blanket but immediately dismissed the idea. If he had learned nothing else over the past several months, he had certainly learned that asking questions and breaking even the smallest of rules was a devastatingly bad idea.

Two days and two nights came and went for Oliver inside the ring of the powerhouse jail. On the morning of the third day, his name was called and he was escorted back to Butler Cottage.

"Well, that sure learned me a lesson," Oliver mumbled under his breath. He never thought he would be so happy to see his housemates and his own real mattress!

For the rest of that winter, Oliver managed to keep from getting into any further trouble. He followed every rule to the very letter. He wore one shirt and one pair of knickers – no matter what. He made his bed each morning without so much as a single wrinkle. He completed his chores without skipping any steps and always finished on time. His meals were eaten in silence, never commenting on the taste and never asking for seconds.

As winter slowly turned to spring, Oliver looked forward each day to the half hour that the boys were allowed to be on the playground. He loved swinging on the swings, tipping his head back as far as he could with his eyes closed. It made him feel like he hadn't a care in the world. He could pretend that his life was very different as long as his eyes were closed. Sometimes he imagined that he was back on East 19th Street helping his father push the suit racks. He imagined his sister, Anna, helping his mother in the kitchen and little Edward standing in his crib. Sometimes he pretended that he was someone else altogether… someone who lived in a fancy house with a loving mother and father… someone who had one of those bicycles he had seen so long ago from the Guarish Society window. It was fun pretending.

It was just one such spring day that Oliver and his housemates watched as a tall, skinny kid that everyone called 'Daddy Long Legs,' took off like a shot from the playground. He was trying to run away, and in fact, he almost succeeded. Secretly, the boys on the playground cheered him on. Within just ten minutes though, the boys could see across the field to where the runaway was being escorted by two guards back to the orphanage, hands held behind his back.

As the boys stood silent, Oliver called out, "Hi Daddy Long Legs!"

The other boys sounded an audible gasp as one of the guards ran over and took Oliver by the scruff of the neck, dragging him away with the runaway.

* * * *

"Now *that one* cost me a whole week in that powerhouse jail!" Oliver said out loud on the train to no one but Edward, who had fallen back asleep alongside his big brother. "A whole week just for saying that!"

CHAPTER SIX

The Orphans Ride West

Oliver sat up straight, nudging Edward. "Wake up, it's time to eat!" he whispered to his sleepy brother. Edward rubbed his eyes and leaned his head into the aisle to see what was going on. The matron smiled as she handed each child a mustard sandwich and a tin cup of milk.

"Pretty good sandwich, huh Edward?" Oliver asked his brother, offering a cheerful smile.

Edward raised his eyes to Oliver as he bit into his sandwich, his head bobbing up and down in approval. Wondering again about what was ahead for them, Oliver thought about their last day at the orphanage...

* * * *

"Give me your attention boys," Matron O'Brien commanded as she stood over the table at last night's supper. "There has been a decision made by the Children's Aid Society that affects many of the children living here at The Children's Village. It seems that due to overcrowding, many of you are going to be resettled with families in the Western Territory. If your name is called, you are to meet your escort in front of the Administration Building immediately after the morning meal."

Oliver watched as Matron O'Brien read from her notepad. He was startled to hear his own name called since he had only been listening half-heartedly. He never expected that she would be talking about him. Now where had she said they were going? Did she mention how long they would be there? He knew he didn't dare ask any questions, and since he did hear her say to go to the Administration Building after breakfast tomorrow, he decided he would just do that. He'd have to figure the rest out later.

On the morning of March 31, 1908, Oliver arrived with four of his housemates at the big Administration Building of The Children's Village Orphanage. He was surprised to see about thirty other children clustered about the front lawn. There were boys of all ages – even a few babies in the arms of several matrons. Before long, a man who introduced himself as their escort, Reverend Swan, began to read off their names.

"I wonder what an escort is?" Oliver considered to himself.

That thought was quickly replaced by the call of, "Oliver Nordmark... Edward Nordmark..."

Oliver could not believe his ears. Edward was here too! Frantically, Oliver began to look around among the crowd trying to locate his brother. Weaving in and around the other children, he finally spotted Edward at the side of a matron who held one of the babies. No longer looking like a baby himself, Edward had grown quite a bit in the year since Oliver had last seen him, but there was no mistaking those dimpled cheeks – it was Edward alright!

Quickly taking him by the hand, Oliver looked up very matter-of-factly at the matron and announced, "I'm Oliver Nordmark, Edward's big brother."

The matron cast a downward glance at Oliver. She dropped Edward's hand saying, "Oh good. You keep a hold of him and see that he doesn't get separated from the group."

Oliver spent the next few minutes reacquainting himself with Edward who seemed a bit surprised at this change of guardians. Ever so slowly, the surprise was replaced with a faint recognition of a face from the past. After all, a year seems like a lifetime when you're just six years old!

Before long, the children were being led to two horse-drawn flatbed wagons. They climbed aboard to begin the first leg of the journey that surely would change their lives. Oliver sat with Edward between his legs. So many conflicting feelings and emotions were welling up inside him. He was scared... he was sad... he was thrilled to have Edward back at his side... he was apprehensive that perhaps the two of them would be separated again... he was excited to discover what might lie ahead for them. Quietly to himself, Oliver made his decision. He would stick with being excited about the possible adventures to come. After all, nothing ventured, nothing gained. Isn't that what his father had always said? Ah, his father... Oliver hoped that his father would be proud of him for taking Edward under his wing. He hoped his mum, who Oliver imagined must be an angel by now, would watch out for her boys and keep them out of harm's way.

After a short wagon ride, the orphans pulled into the crowded train station. There were other children there as well. Both boys and girls would be making this journey. Oliver thought of his sister, Anna, as his eyes darted about, searching, but Anna was nowhere to be found. The boys from the wagons were led to the passenger car at the back of the train. They climbed aboard and settled into the soft leather seats, filled with anticipation and just a bit of worry.

CHAPTER SEVEN

Kansas or Bust!

As they awoke on the third day of their journey west, Oliver and Edward made a pact.

"We have to stay together, no matter what," said Oliver.

"No matter what," Edward repeated.

"You're not a baby anymore, Edward. So if they split up the babies from the boys, you're a big boy now," Oliver reasoned out loud. "You let me do the talking."

"Oliver talks," echoed Edward.

Later that day, after another lunch of mustard sandwiches and warm milk, things seemed like they were about to change.

Reverend Swan walked slowly down the center of the train announcing, "We'll be pulling into Nemaha County Station in about fifteen minutes. Now you children get yourselves together and looking your best for the townspeople. Get those shirt tails tucked in and pull your socks up, and for Heaven's sake, make sure you don't have any dirt on your faces!" Their escort turned and walked back to the front of the passenger car leaving the children exchanging questioning glances.

Turner Hall – Bern Opera House

Slowly, the words of instruction began to sink in and everyone began the task of 'getting themselves together.' There were no mirrors, so the children took turns spit shining one another's faces until they were satisfied that each was looking his best.

When the whistle blew, announcing the train's arrival at the Nemaha County Station, the boys and girls crowded against the windows for a glimpse of their destination. Stopping at the platform, the children were led off the train and onto waiting wagons.

"Stay close by me now, Edward," warned Oliver.

Edward followed his big brother's command, staying so close that he bumped into Oliver's leg with every step. The two of them climbed aboard the wagon, heads tossing left and right, trying to take in all the sights.

This was a small town with dirt roads and wooden buildings. Each building had a wood pole staked out across the front. Some of the poles had horses tied to them. There were people walking about and children running in the street playing games with sticks and round hoops. The wagons took the orphans to the far end of town where there stood a big building. Wide steps led up to the big front doors. Across the top of the doors, Oliver could read the words TURNER HALL – BERN OPERA HOUSE. Just under that he read out loud to no one, "Bern, Kansas." A sign nailed to the side of the door read, VAUDEVILLE PERFORMANCE FIRST SATURDAY OF EVERY MONTH. In front of the building there were many horse-drawn buggies, flatbed wagons and carts.

"What do we do?" asked a worried Edward.

"Just stay close to me. Here, take my hand," replied Oliver as he slipped his hand into Edward's. "Don't worry Edward, and remember, you're not a baby. You're a boy."

Edward followed Oliver up the wide steps of the Opera House, then through the big doors. Once inside, the boys filed along a table where a gentleman asked their names and their ages.

"Oliver Nordmark. I'm nearly ten," Oliver stated loudly. The gentleman wrote Oliver's name and age on a piece of paper attached to a string.

"Around your neck with this," the man instructed. "Next?"

"Edward Nordmark," began Edward as he tried to sound just like Oliver. "I'm six, so I'm a boy, not a baby."

"Well, indeed you are," replied the man with a smile. "Welcome to Kansas, Edward." He handed Edward his name and age on a paper like Oliver's and Edward quickly placed it around his neck.

"I'm *not* a baby," Edward repeated under his breath, as he followed Oliver and the other children onto the stage of the Opera House. There were chairs on the stage and the boys quickly sat down, looking all around and wondering what would happen next. Within minutes they had their answer.

After all the children were seated, men and women came into the Opera House and began walking up and down in front of the boys and girls, looking them over. Some asked questions, others just looked. One girl, who sat a few seats down from Oliver, began reciting a poem to the townspeople, trying to make a good impression. Eventually, a farmer and his wife stopped in front of Oliver and Edward.

"Are you brothers?" the man asked with a strong foreign accent.

"Yes," replied Oliver, "and we're staying together because I'm in charge of Edward." Oliver tried his hardest to sound firm and very grown up. "His matron put me in charge of him when we left New York City, and that was three days ago."

"Well, then I suppose we are both very lucky today. We are looking for two brothers to live on our farm and help us with the farm chores. I think that you two boys would make a fine choice," the farmer said with a smile.

He turned to his wife and quickly spoke a foreign language to her. She looked at Oliver and Edward, nodded her head, then turned to the farmer and answered him in the same strange tongue.

"Then it is settled," the farmer spoke in English. "Come with us boys."

Edward and Oliver rose from their seats, grinning to one another at their success at having been able to stay together.

CHAPTER EIGHT

Farm Boys in Kansas

"I am Henry Blauer," began the farmer as he spoke to Oliver and Edward who sat close together in the back of the flatbed wagon.

The horse-drawn wagon, loaded with supplies from the General Store, rattled down the rocky path away from the little town of Bern, Kansas. The boys held tight to the sides of the wagon, and to each other, to keep from sliding about.

"This is my wife, Mattie," the farmer continued, "but you will call her Mrs. Blauer."

"Yes Sir," replied Oliver.

"We are here in this country from our motherland, Switzerland, you see," said farmer Blauer. "We are farming the land and raising animals for food. We have horses, hogs, chickens, and goats," he continued in his strong German accent. "There are many chores, and since we have no children of our own, we need strong boys to help. Do you know how to do this farm work, boys?"

Oliver was dumbstruck. Not only did he have no clue about farm work, he had never even been near a farm. Of course he knew about horses, but he had never seen hogs, chickens or goats. He could remember eating chicken, but he was pretty sure that wouldn't count. What kind of chores could possibly have to do with chickens?

"Ah... well... not too much," Oliver finally managed to say, "but I'm sure me and Edward will learn real quick! We're good learners, that's for sure!"

Eventually, the Blauer's horse and wagon turned onto a long lane. Peering out the sides, Oliver and Edward looked off in the distance. They saw a house on one side of the lane, and a big red barn on the other. There were wooden pens around the barn and a smaller building, like a miniature barn, between the house and the big barn.

"What's that small barn for?" Oliver asked excitedly.

"Now that is the chicken coop," replied Mrs. Blauer. "One of your chores will be to gather the eggs that the chickens lay. Come with me," she said as the wagon pulled to a stop at the end of the lane. "I'll show you just what I mean."

All set for their newest adventure, Oliver and Edward climbed over the sides of the wagon and raced each other to the chicken coop. Just outside the door of the coop, the boys found a wire pen that was full of baby chicks. Unable to contain his excitement, Oliver reached in and picked up a baby chick.

"Fly little birdie, fly!" he exclaimed, as he tossed the chick into the air as high as he could.

Much to Oliver and Edward's dismay, the chick did not fly. Instead, it came crashing to the ground at the boy's feet and lay lifeless in the dirt.

"Oh, you little street urchin!" said Mrs. Blauer in disgust. "You stupid, stupid boy! A baby chick does not fly like a bird!" She stormed off into the farmhouse leaving the boys and Mr. Blauer standing alone with the fallen chick.

Oliver felt just terrible. He had no idea that baby chicks could not fly. All of a sudden, he did not feel so good about this farm adventure anymore.

"They were so cute," Oliver began in explanation to Mr. Blauer. "I was just gonna teach it to fly. You can bet I won't do that anymore. I feel so bad for that baby chick."

"You'll learn," replied Mr. Blauer as he bent and scooped up the dead chick. "You'll learn."

* * * *

Early the next morning, Oliver and Edward were surprised to be woken from a deep sleep at 5:00 AM.

"Come along boys," shouted Mrs. Blauer. "Out of your bed now. There is much work to do."

Rubbing their eyes with the backs of their hands, the boys pushed off the blanket and stretched their legs to meet the wooden floor. Finding their way down the stairs to the kitchen, Oliver and Edward saw two bowls of oatmeal on the table.

"Go and wash up now you two," Mrs. Blauer directed. "You will not be eating at my table with dirty hands."

"Yes, Mrs. Blauer," the boys replied in unison.

After a quick washing at the water pump, the boys settled down to their first breakfast in their new home. Adding lots of sugar, Oliver and Edward took little time finishing what Mrs. Blauer had put in their bowls.

"Alright then boys, follow me now," called Mrs. Blauer over her shoulder as she exited the kitchen.

Oliver and Edward dutifully followed as Mrs. Blauer led them to the chicken coop.

"Your first task every morning will be to collect the eggs from the chickens," began Mrs. Blauer. "First, you chase any chickens from the coop into the yard." She demonstrated as she shooed at the chickens. "Next, you carefully gather the eggs into your baskets. Every week you will clean the chicken coop. You will remove the manure and wipe down the perches. Do you see these small bugs?" she questioned.

Two small heads nodded up and down.

"These are mites," Mrs. Blauer stated. "You must paint these with a brush dipped into the creosote bucket over there. It is the only way to kill them."

"Yuck," thought Oliver.

"Yuck," said Edward out loud.

"Remember, every week this must be done," repeated Mrs. Blauer. "Now get to work!" She turned and left the chicken coop, leaving Oliver and Edward alone.

"Well Edward, let's get to work then," said Oliver with a smile. "We're farmers now, and this is farmer's work. I think it looks like fun."

Slowly the boys got the hang of gathering the eggs and gently placing them in their baskets. They cleaned up the droppings with small metal shovels they found sticking out of a bucket in the corner of the coop. They cleaned off the perches as best they could with an old rag, then carefully began the task of painting the creosote onto the perches. It left a bad smell and the boys were anxious to be finished and get out of there.

"Hey, Edward," whispered Oliver as they reached the back of the chicken coop. "I got an idea!"

"What?" wondered Edward aloud.

"Put an egg in each of your pockets, like this," began Oliver. "Leave your basket here and follow me!"

Edward followed Oliver's lead and tucked an egg deep into each of his pockets then hurried to catch up with his big brother. Running around to the back of the big barn where no one would see them, Oliver and Edward took turns tossing the eggs as high as they could against the side of the barn. Laughing and giggling, they watched as the yellow yolks ran down the side of the big red barn.

"Maybe there's something to this farm life after all!" laughed Oliver as he and Edward smiled at each other.

"Yep!" replied Edward. "This is fun being farmers!"

* * * *

The next morning was sunny and hot. Oliver and Edward quickly rushed through breakfast and out to gather the eggs from the chicken coop. They had intended to have some more fun behind the barn, but on their way, they heard a strange noise.

"Woo, Woo, Woo Woo," came the noise from the back of the barn.

"What was that?" Edward asked tentatively.

"Let's go see!" answered Oliver, who was always looking for adventure.

Walking through the barn, they continued to hear the strange noise. When they reached the back of the barn, they saw a pen full of short fat animals.

"What are them animals, Oliver?" Edward asked.

"I think they must be hogs, but I don't know for sure. I never seen a real hog before," Oliver replied. "Hey, I got an idea Edward. Come on!"

The boys ran back into the barn and picked up some long slats that were used to cover cracks on the barn walls. Quietly they snuck into the pen of hogs and started poking and chasing them around and around.

"Woo, Woo Woo," squealed the hogs, making quite a racket.

Mr. and Mrs. Blauer came running out of the farmhouse. At just that very minute, Reverend Swan, the man from New York who had escorted the boys on the train, pulled up in a horse-drawn buggy. He was stopping by to check on the boys before he left town. Seeing the panic on the Blauer's faces, he jumped from his buggy and joined them in their race to the barn.

"Oliver! Edward!" shouted Mr. Blauer. "Stop that right now, do you hear me?"

The boys ended their chase and tossed down their boards. Unfortunately, it was too late for the largest of the hogs. The heat of the sun and the chasing around was just too much. The hog plopped himself down in a mud puddle and died.

"Ahh!" gasped Oliver and Edward, alarmed at this latest development.

They looked at the Blauers and Reverend Swan with their innocent faces, for surely, they had no idea that running would cause a hog to die.

Oliver leaned slightly in Edward's direction and whispered, "We might just get a whippin' for this Edward."

CHAPTER NINE

Life Turns Again

Much to Oliver's surprise, there was no whipping issued for hog chasing that day. The brothers were, however, admonished for their behavior and told not to do anything like that again. They were immediately sent into a nearby field to pull weeds – pigweed it was called – that would be used as feed for the hogs.

Oliver and Edward tried hard to enjoy themselves on the Kansas farm. There were many chores and the boys often went to bed exhausted and without enough to eat, but somehow they always found a way to have a little fun.

About six months after their arrival and placement at the Blauer's farm, Oliver began to notice things that set his mind thinking. He felt no real affection from his guardians. In fact, the Blauers were often angry and annoyed with their new charges – especially Mrs. Blauer.

"You boys come down here for your lunch right now or there will be no food for you," Mrs. Blauer called up the stairs, one cold winter afternoon.

It was Saturday, and the boys had finished their morning chores early. They had retreated to their room to get out of the cold and had just started a game of marbles on the wooden floor when the shouting started. Knowing that she meant business, and knowing that there would be more chores after lunch, Oliver and Edward quickly pushed their game under the bed and ran down to the kitchen.

"Now eat that," said Mrs. Blauer as she pushed two tin bowls of soup in front of the boys, "then get yourselves out to the barn and clean those stalls. There's plenty more to do when that's done, so don't waste time."

Looking down at the grease floating on top of the soup, Oliver remembered what he had learned in the orphanage and checked his tongue. He knew better than to complain about food, or even to ask questions for that matter. Edward, on the other hand, had not learned this lesson.

"This is bad! I don't like it," he whined.

Taking Edward by the hair, Mrs. Blauer pushed his face towards the bowl and snarled, "You'll eat it and be thankful that you have anything to eat at all!"

Silently, Edward began eating the soup, glancing up at Oliver with a sick look on his face. Oliver, too, continued to eat the greasy soup. About halfway through his bowl, Oliver felt his stomach churning. Rushing from his seat, he headed straight to the coal bucket in the corner and vomited. His chest heaved and his throat felt as though it would choke as the retching continued. Finally, as the agony began to subside, Oliver stumbled back to his seat.

"You don't like the soup? That's fine, you can eat with the dogs!" shouted a very angry Mrs. Blauer.

Oliver couldn't believe his ears. He knew exactly what the six dogs that lived on the Blauer's farm ate. At butchering time, the rinds were saved. The lard was boiled out of the rinds and food scraps and corn meal were stirred in to make dog food.

Slowly, Edward and Oliver rose from the table and went to the pantry. Old brown paper scraps were kept there to feed the dogs on. Oliver went into the pantry first and retrieved a paper. As he left the pantry with his head down, Edward went to get his paper. Not being able to face eating dog food, little Edward glanced up and saw the pantry window. Without even thinking, he pushed open the sash and climbed out into the cold. As soon as his feet hit the ground, he took off like a shot in the direction of town. Mrs. Blauer waited only a few seconds then followed Edward into the pantry.

Seeing the open window, she stuck her head out and bellowed, "You come back here or I'll get the hounds after you!"

Poor little Edward! He was afraid of the dogs when they were standing still – he was petrified of being chased by them. Crying and sobbing, tears streaming down his face, Edward turned and ran back to the house.

Mrs. Blauer changed her mind about the boys eating with the dogs that day. Instead, she handed each boy a crust of bread and shooed them out to the barn to begin their afternoon chores.

* * * *

The only respite that Edward and Oliver got from the Blauers was the time they spent in school. Shortly after their arrival in Kansas, Mr. Blauer had taken the boys to the schoolhouse to begin their studies. Riding in the back of the farmer's wagon, Oliver and Edward enjoyed looking around at their new surroundings, breathing in the fresh clean air. When the first school day came to an end, the brothers ran from the building expecting to see Mr. Blauer's wagon to take them home. Not seeing their ride, they sat down under a nearby tree to wait. No wagon arrived and finally their new teacher, Mrs. Kelly, came out of the schoolhouse.

"What are you two boys up to, just sitting there?" she asked.

"We're waitin' for our wagon ride home," explained Oliver.

"I'd say your waiting is over. It doesn't seem that a wagon is coming for you, so you'd better start walking," Mrs. Kelly replied as she turned and disappeared around the corner of the building.

Oliver and Edward looked at one another, shrugged their shoulders and got up to start the trek home. Oliver soon began to regret not paying closer attention to the route they had taken to school that morning. They climbed a gently sloping hill, then walked along the top of that hill for quite a distance.

"How much further?" complained Edward. "I'm tired and my feet hurt!"

"Not too much further," Oliver lied.

Coming down the other side of the hill, they walked through a little valley and then came to a crick.

"We didn't cross no crick in the wagon, Oliver," warned Edward. "You got us lost!"

"I know we didn't cross a crick, Edward. We're taking a short cut," lied Oliver again. "Now stop complaining and keep up with me!"

Finding a place that seemed shallow enough to cross, Edward and Oliver made their way across stepping stones, trying hard to keep their shoes dry. The other side of the crick was quite rugged, and the boys stumbled repeatedly but kept moving on.

Finally, they came to a wagon path that, to Oliver, looked somewhat familiar. Taking a chance, he decided that they would follow that path.

After what seemed like hours, they arrived dusty and exhausted at a turn in the path that Oliver was now *sure* he recognized.

"This way, Edward!" he shouted as he began to run with renewed energy.

"Wait for me!" Edward moaned as he too began to run to keep up with his big brother. "Don't leave me!"

At last the boys arrived back at the Blauer's farm. Running up to Mr. Blauer outside the chicken coop, Oliver expected the man to be very apologetic for having forgotten to retrieve them.

"Now that took you longer than it should have," began farmer Blauer. "Next time, get yourselves straight back here after school. There's chores to do, you know. It shouldn't be taking you that long to walk just one mile."

"One mile!" thought Oliver. "*Just* one mile?"

The boys both paid closer attention the following morning on their wagon ride to school. This time they found their way back with no trouble when classes had ended. By the end of the week, they were walking both ways and enjoying their time alone together.

* * * *

As much as they enjoyed their time going to and from school, being at school was sometimes hard for Oliver and Edward. Since they spoke differently than the other children, because of their New York accents, they were often picked on and made fun of.

"Hey, city boys!" taunted a particularly mean boy one morning in the schoolyard. "No one ever taught you to speak English straight? I guess no one to teach ya, bein' as you got no ma or pa."

Laughter and snickering erupted from the small crowd of boys encircling the brothers.

"Oh yeah? Who says I can't speak English?" Oliver fumed back at the bully. "This should speak clearly enough!" he shouted as he lunged forward, swinging his tin lunch bucket towards the offender.

The bully took the hit square on his left knee and as he started to stagger, Oliver dropped the bucket and dove onto the boy with fists flying. Just as Oliver was clearly getting the better of his opponent, Mrs. Kelly saw what was happening and came running.

"Stop that fighting now!" she commanded. "Do you hear me? I said NOW!" She tugged at the boys, who broke apart from one another, eyes glaring. "There will be no more of that from the two of you. If there is, it will mean expulsion. Now inside with all of you."

The boys headed for the schoolhouse with Oliver and Edward lagging behind.

"You really showed him, Oliver!" Edward praised his brother. "You were winning that fight, that's for sure!"

Oliver just shrugged his shoulders and followed Edward inside. Although they continued to be picked on now and again, everyone knew not to push it too hard. Oliver had proven that he wasn't afraid of any of them, and he would fight for himself and for his brother if that was what he had to do.

* * * *

During the bitter cold January of 1909, something happened that convinced Oliver that things were going to change for him and Edward. After their morning trek to school, the boys watched with their classmates from the schoolhouse windows as the skies took on a menacing shade of gray. Before long, the dark clouds had opened up and swirling snow began to fall. The students were all excited as they dreamed of the fun they would have in the snow once school was out. As the hours wore on, the winds picked up and the snow fell harder and harder. Looking warily out at the storm, Mrs. Kelly made a quick decision.

"Class dismissed students," she announced. "We'll all need time to get home before this storm becomes dangerous."

Cheering shouts erupted from the class as all the students jumped from their seats and raced from the schoolhouse. Once outside, the sheering winds ripped right through Oliver and Edward as they anxiously looked around, hoping to see farmer Blauer. Seeing no one, and seeing no wagon in sight, they did the only thing they knew to do.

"Pull your stocking cap down as far as it will go, Edward," Oliver instructed. "We're going to have to start walking. I'm sure farmer Blauer will be along shortly. He's probably trying to get through the snow right now."

"But he doesn't know that school ended early," Edward said in protest. "He's not coming for us. He never comes for us."

Oliver considered this possibility but quickly dismissed it. "This is a blizzard, Edward. Even farmer Blauer knows we could never walk a mile home in a blizzard. He'll come. Let's get started. We'll stay warmer if we're moving. We'll freeze if we just stand here waiting."

Even though he wasn't really following Oliver's reasoning, Edward fell in behind his brother as the two boys started the trip home. It wasn't long before they could see nothing ahead of them and nothing behind them. The schoolhouse disappeared in the flying snow. The wind was blowing so strongly that Oliver could hardly see ten feet in front of himself. The only way he knew where he was going was to watch the ridge of the hill, and then to follow the river bank of the crick. Edward held tight to the back of

Oliver's coat so as not to get separated in the storm. Both boys felt frozen to the core.

"We're going to die in the snow, Oliver!" Edward cried.

"No, we won't die, but we *are* cold, Edward. When farmer Blauer finds us, he'll take us to the farmhouse and warm us with hot coffee," replied Oliver.

Secretly, Oliver did not believe a word of his comfort to Edward. Although he found it nearly impossible to believe, he instinctively knew that no one was coming for them. No one ever came for them... not even in a blizzard.

Finally making it to the Blauer's farmhouse, Oliver and Edward fell exhausted and freezing through the front door.

"Come on now, boys!" Mrs. Blauer called out. "Get those wet things off before they drip all over everything."

Oliver could not believe his ears. No apology... no concern... no comfort.

"The only one looking out for us, is us," Oliver thought. "Now there's a lesson I've finally learned. We're on our own, whether we live on this farm or in New York City. We're on our own." It was a lesson that Oliver would remember until the day he died.

CHAPTER TEN

Don't Forget Me Edward

Slowly, the deep cold of winter began to fade. The days began to get longer, and little signs of spring started popping up all around the farm. As Oliver and Edward watched farmer Blauer begin to till the soil for the spring planting, Oliver had the idea that he wanted to plant a garden of his own.

"I have no seed to spare for such folly," farmer Blauer replied when Oliver went to him for some seeds to plant.

"If I find some seeds of my own, can I plant them?" Oliver asked hopefully.

"I don't know where you would find any, but if you do, yes, you can plant them behind the chicken coop," the farmer replied.

"Now where can I find seeds?" wondered Oliver.

He thought about planting kernels of corn, but he decided that probably wouldn't work. Maybe he could plant cucumber seeds. But what would be the sense in that? Even if they did grow, Oliver didn't like cucumbers. No, he wanted to plant something that would grow just for him and Edward to eat. Cantaloupe! That's what he would plant. Both Oliver and Edward loved the sweet taste of fresh cantaloupe. The next morning, when cantaloupe was on the breakfast table, Oliver put his plan into motion.

"I'd be happy to help cut that cantaloupe, Mrs. Blauer," offered Oliver. "I'm getting bigger now, and I can handle a cutting knife."

Mrs. Blauer looked suspiciously towards Oliver. Not imagining what he could be up to, and not caring to do more than necessary for the boys, she nodded her head yes.

Oliver jumped from his seat and carefully took the sharp knife into his hand. Very slowly, he pushed the knife through the center of the fruit and gently separated the two halves. When he was sure that Mrs. Blauer wasn't looking, Oliver scooped a handful of the seeds from the cantaloupe and quickly slid them into his pocket. Of course, he wasn't sure if he would get in trouble, should she see him, but you could never tell with Mrs. Blauer. Best to be on the safe side and not let her see, Oliver reasoned.

Shortly before lunch, when the morning chores had been completed, Oliver had some free time. He ran behind the chicken coop with his pocketful of seeds and began to dig with one of the shovels from the coop.

"Watcha up to?" Edward asked.

"Oh, Edward, you scared me!" a startled Oliver replied. "I'm making a garden of cantaloupe just for me and you."

"When can we eat them?" Edward wanted to know.

"It'll take a while for them to grow," Oliver answered. "I'm not really sure, but probably sometime in the summer."

"Can I help?" asked Edward.

Oliver smiled, handing Edward his shovel as he ran into the chicken coop for a second one. The boys worked busily on their garden. They planted the seeds in rows, carefully covering and watering them. Oliver got some old chicken wire from the coop and pushed it into the ground, all around their little garden.

"That should do it," Oliver proudly stated as he and Edward stood back to look at their work.

"Yep! That should do it," Edward repeated.

Smiling at one another, the boys ran off towards the farmhouse for lunch.

* * * *

Every day, for the next few weeks, Oliver would sneak behind the chicken coop to check on his garden. He was elated the morning he saw tiny green sprouts reaching up through the soil. Spring gradually turned to summer and the sprouts grew into small vines stretching out across the earth. Oliver was anxious and excited to see if his plants would actually bear fruit.

* * * *

On the morning of July 27, 1909, Oliver and Edward woke to some unexpected news.

"Out of bed you two," Mrs. Blauer nudged the boys. "That man from the Children's Aid Society is on his way for you right now, so get ready."

"Ready for what?" a groggy Oliver asked.

"He's taking you back on the train to find a different place to live. We can't keep you here any longer," Mrs. Blauer said flatly.

Without a word, Oliver and Edward rose from their bed and quickly dressed for the day. They reached under the bed for their small carrying case and haphazardly stuffed their few belongings into it. The boys stumbled down the stairs to the kitchen and quietly ate their breakfast. Once finished, they walked outside and sat stiffly on the front step of the farmhouse.

"Where will we go?" Edward wanted to know.

"I don't know, Edward," replied Oliver, as he looked slowly around the Blauer farm, "but wherever it is, I bet it will be better than living here."

"Can we take our garden with us?" Edward asked, as he looked sadly towards the chicken coop.

"No Edward, you can't carry a garden with you."

"We'll stick together, right Oliver?"

"We're brothers, Edward. We'll stick together," Oliver reassured him.

Before long, the horse-drawn buggy from the Children's Aid Society pulled into the farmhouse lane and the boys stood up, holding their belongings.

"Come along boys, climb in," said Reverend Swan, trying to sound cheery.

Silently, Oliver and Edward climbed into the buggy. As it pulled away from the Blauer farm, Oliver looked over his shoulder expecting to wave goodbye, but Mrs. Blauer never came out of the house. Looking towards the barn, Oliver could see farmer Blauer feeding the hogs. He never looked up as the buggy went by. If he had, he would have seen two quiet and frightened boys huddled together, trying to become one.

* * * *

The buggy carried Oliver and Edward back to the town of Bern. It stopped at the train station where the man instructed the boys to gather their things and come with him.

"The train will be coming for you soon," said Reverend Swan. "You'll ride with more children further west. The next stop will be Mankato, about a hundred and fifty miles, I'd say."

Not knowing what to say, the boys silently awaited the train's arrival. They climbed aboard and settled in for the hundred and fifty mile trek.

Arriving in Mankato, Oliver and Edward followed very much the same routine as they had upon their arrival in Bern, Kansas a year before. They lined up on the Opera House stage with their name tags around their necks and waited to be chosen by one of the farmers or merchants now inspecting the children.

"I'm Frank McCammon," a gruff voice announced in Oliver's direction. "I think you'll do just fine." He placed a hand on Oliver's shoulder, but Oliver jerked back in his seat.

"Me and Edward are brothers, and we're stayin' together," Oliver boldly announced, figuring he had nothing to lose.

"Well, I'm afraid I've got no use for a young one like him," Mr. McCammon replied, glancing in Edward's direction. "He couldn't do the kind of work I've got in mind."

As Edward's face flushed in fear and tears began to fill the corners of his eyes, an old man poked his head into their conversation.

"Well Frank, I reckon I could take the little fellow home with me. You're not more than a day's ride from my place. I'm sure we could let the boys visit with each other now and again," spoke the older farmer.

"Name's Gish. William Gish. But you can just call me Gish," he introduced himself to Edward with an extended right hand.

Taking the wrinkled hand in his, Edward heard himself softly say, "I'm Edward Nordmark."

"Well then Edward, have we got a deal?" William Gish asked with a smile.

Looking towards his brother, Edward searched for the answer in Oliver's eyes. As his heart sank, Oliver nodded in Edward's direction. He knew that these people could separate them no matter what Oliver and Edward wanted, and at least these two farmers lived fairly close to one another. If Edward didn't find a home here in Mankato and had to get back on the train, there would be no telling how far apart the two of them would be.

"It's a deal," Oliver spoke up for his brother. "But only if we get to see each other at least four times a year."

Both farmers nodded their agreement, and the four of them headed off the stage. They stopped at the desk, where the local committee recorded the new placements, then walked out of the Opera House. As their wagons headed off in different directions, Oliver tried to stay brave for little Edward.

"Don't forget me, Edward!" he called out to farmer Gish's wagon with a forced smile. "Never forget me!"

CHAPTER ELEVEN

Oliver on His Own

F rank McCammon's wagon traveled ten miles west of Mankato that
day to his farm in Esbon, Kansas. William Gish's wagon headed south
for twelve miles to Ionia, Kansas. Despite their agreement in the Opera
House, Oliver and Edward visited with one another only one time over
the next four years. Oliver spent those years as a farm hand. He worked
hard, learning all the skills needed to be a successful farmer.

The McCammon's treated Oliver well. When he first arrived at their
farm, Frank's wife, Hettie, took Oliver shopping for new clothes – a first
for Oliver. He was baptized at the Mt. Zion Church just before his 11th
birthday. Frank McCammon was a prominent citizen in Esbon. His
brother John was the postmaster in 1906 and Frank clerked for the
mayor in 1907. Their family was one of the first to settle Esbon in 1887,
and they had many successful businesses. The McCammon one-room
schoolhouse (renamed Mt. Zion School in 1919) was located at the
corner of their farm, just six miles from town.

Four times a year, Oliver received a letter from either Reverend Swan or Reverend Brace of the Children's Aid Society asking how he was doing in his new home. Each time, Oliver would write back with the details of his life. He wrote about what he was learning in school, what chores he did on the farm, and his plans for his future. He always asked about his brother Edward, but neither Reverend Swan nor Reverend Brace ever responded to that question, leaving Oliver to wonder and worry.

Oliver Nordmark on horseback with Frank McCammon

* * * *

On July 4, 1913, Oliver Nordmark, who was just shy of his fifteenth birthday, rose as usual before the sun. He strapped on his overalls and headed to the barn for the morning milking. He met up with Mr. McCammon outside the barn when the milking was complete.

"Come and help me hitch up my wagon, Oliver," McCammon called out. "My wife and I are headed up to my brother's place for a visit. When you're done with all your chores, you're welcome to go into town and meet up with your friends. There's going to be a big 4th of July celebration, you know. Maybe even some fireworks."

"Sure thing," replied Oliver, excited at the idea of having some fun. "I'll get everything done."

Oliver watched as the wagon carrying McCammon and his wife pulled off. He quickly turned to get started with the day's work. He fed and watered McCammon's dog, fed the hogs and cows, mucked out the horse stalls, and cleaned the perches of the chicken coop. It was nearly noon before he had everything finished.

Oliver had a pony in the barn, and he headed off to saddle her up. She wasn't *really* Oliver's pony, but for the time being, she might as well be. McCammon's brother actually owned the pony. She was rather stunted and would never get very big, so he had asked Oliver to break the horse in for his young son to ride. Oliver agreed to the task. He kept the pony in the barn and was real nice to her. He gave her the best hay he could find and plenty of grain. He kept the pony clean and brushed her often. To break the pony for riding, Oliver first put just the saddle blanket on her. After a while, he put the saddle on top of the blanket and let her walk around with it on her back for many days. Eventually, he took to riding the pony. She settled down rather quickly to the feel of Oliver on her back, and soon he was riding the pony all over. McCammon's brother hadn't yet come to take the pony back, and Oliver wasn't about to offer to give her up. And so it was on that July 4th afternoon, young Oliver Nordmark saddled up his pony and headed into town.

* * * *

It was a seven mile ride into Esbon, and Oliver rode like the wind to get there as fast as he could. He quickly met up with some of the boys he knew from school, who had also come to town for the festivities.

"Hey, Oliver!" called out a lanky boy by the name of Guy Ball. "Hitch up that sorry excuse for a horse of yours and get down here. We're fixin' to have a little fun!"

"Be right there, and watch what you say about my pony. She can outrun anything you might be ridin'!" Oliver joked as he headed for the livery stable.

After dismounting and checking in with the stable hand, Oliver ran off to join his friends.

"Come on," Guy motioned to the boys, "let's get us each a cigar to celebrate!"

Into the General Store they went. Oliver looked around, knowing he only had about half a dollar in his pocket. He was feeling a bit hungry but decided to save his money and just get a cigar with his friends. After each boy made his purchase, they headed out behind the shops and down over a small embankment to walk along the crick.

"What took you so long gettin' into town, Oliver?" asked his friend Cliff Horne.

"Oh, you know, McCammon had to go visit his brother which left all the work for me. I got things done just as quick as I could, but I gotta tell you, he's gettin' lazier all the time. If it weren't for me, I bet that whole farm would come fallin' down around him."

"So get out," Guy offered. "If I was you, I'd run off and look to stake out my own claim. He ain't got no hold on you. He ain't your pa or nothin'."

"That he ain't," mused Oliver as he took a .22 revolver from inside his jacket.

"Now how in the blazes did you get that?" gasped Cliff. "You steal that or somethin'?"

"No, I didn't steal it," Oliver indignantly replied. "I ordered it from Montgomery Ward – right out of their catalog."

"Oh yeah," replied Cliff, certain that he was lying, "like McCammon would ever let you keep a gun that was delivered to the farm."

Oliver glanced in Guy's direction and noticed him grinning and shuffling his feet in the dirt.

"You're right, Cliff." Oliver smiled, quite full of himself. "That's why I was smart enough to have them send it to Guy's place. This ain't just a pretty face, ya know. Clever, that's me!"

"Okay then, if you're so clever, let me see you hit that piece of fence post on the other side of the crick," challenged Cliff.

Oliver grinned. Raising the revolver straight out in front of him, he slowly took aim and fired off a shot that hit the post square on.

"Nothin' to it," Oliver boasted. "I can hit a matchstick – that is, if you care to hold it!"

"Whooo-Waaa, Whooo-Waaa," sounded the incoming freight train, grabbing the boy's attention.

"Come on!" shouted Guy, running in the direction of the low whistle. "Let's jump it!"

All the boys headed off in the train's direction, trying to catch up with Guy. Reaching the tracks, they ran along with the slowing train. Shoving their cigars between their lips, one by one the boys jumped onto the side of the train.

"We're ridin' the rails!" someone called out in glee.

All at once, as the train slowed to a stop, an idea came into Oliver's head. It hit him hard.

"Geez…" he thought, "here's my chance to get out of here!"

Oliver made up his mind just that quickly. Without a word to his friends, who were laughing and joking about their ride, Oliver ran straight to the General Store.

"A pound of gingersnaps, please?" Oliver asked the clerk. He paid for them, then looked down to see that he had but twenty-three cents left. He quickly shoved the coins into his pocket and ran from the store.

Glancing in the direction of the livery stable, Oliver thought about the pony. He knew he should take her back to McCammon's barn, but if he did that, he was sure to miss his opportunity.

"Sorry 'bout that McCammon," he murmured to himself.

Running towards the train, Oliver crossed the tracks and lay down in the tall grasses. He figured about ten minutes went by before he heard the calling of the freight train's whistle, announcing its departure from the station. Only a moment of hesitation ran through his head as he thought about what he was about to do. He quickly dismissed any thoughts that would have changed his mind. As the freight train slowly began chugging along the tracks away from the platform, Oliver jumped from his hiding place and started chasing the engine.

"I got me a life to lead," he could hear himself saying. "Nothin' ventured, nothin' gained!" With that, Oliver reached up to the steel handles behind the train's locomotive and pulled himself aboard.

The Chicago, Rock Island and Pacific Railroad freight train pulled out of Esbon, Kansas late on the afternoon of July 4, 1913 with young Oliver Nordmark hitched aboard. Although he never saw the town's fireworks that evening, he was certain that he felt as much excitement as any of his friends. Like a bird taking flight, Oliver was eager to find his own way in the world… and maybe even a lost brother.

CHAPTER TWELVE
The Train Traveler

"Hey you, Sonny! Down off that engine!" the railroad cop called out to Oliver. "Get over here!"

The freight train that Oliver had been clinging to through the last three little towns had come to a stop on a siding – a piece of track that allows one train to pull over, letting a second train get by. A fancy passenger train passed by and came to a stop at the platform where waiting travelers began to gather their belongings in preparation to board the train.

Fearing that the railroad cop might pull the gun that Oliver could see gleaming from his holster, the teenager did as he was commanded. With his head lowered, he sheepishly climbed down from his perch just behind the freight train's engine and crossed the tracks. Several railroad cops were gathering up the handful of hobos who had attempted to hitch a ride, free of charge, on the big freight train. Oliver walked slowly, avoiding any eye contact with the cops, to the back of the line.

"There's a cold jail cell waitin' for you freeloaders," one railroad cop called out in disdain.

Glancing behind him, Oliver saw the line of people waiting to board the passenger train, and he quickly came up with a plan. The minute the railroad cops were distracted, he slipped out of his line headed for jail and silently joined the line of paying customers. Oliver reached up and slowly removed his cap, trying to change his appearance. Keeping his eyes away from the line of hobos and standing very still, Oliver counted his lucky stars when he caught a glimpse from the corner of his eye of the hobos marching off to jail. He breathed a long sigh of relief.

As the passengers began shuffling forward to board the train, Oliver scooted out of line and circled around behind the passenger train. Quickly, he darted off in the direction of the freight train. So as not to be seen, he crouched down in the tall grass on the far side of the track and waited patiently for the passenger train to pull out of the station. As the freight train sounded its long, low whistle announcing its departure from the siding, Oliver waited for just the right moment. Running alongside as the train picked up speed, he reached up to the steel handles just behind the engine, pulling himself aboard.

"Whew! That was a close call," Oliver said to himself. "I can't let that happen again. I might not be so lucky the next time."

When the freight train slowed to a crawl through the next several small towns, Oliver would jump off the train and hide in the tall grasses, unseen by the railroad cops. When the train was ready to start up again, Oliver would run alongside and jump back on.

This method of travel was working well until Oliver began to get tired and weak. It was late afternoon, Oliver figured, as he glanced at the sun lowering in the western sky. It wouldn't be too much longer before the sun would disappear off the horizon. Oliver knew he needed a new plan. As the train pulled into another siding to allow a passenger train through to the station, Oliver had an idea.

"I need to quit this freight train," he whispered to himself.

As the train slowed, Oliver dropped from behind the engine and rolled into the tall grass. He hid there quietly while the travelers boarded the passenger train.

"Think... think!" he said to himself. "What'll I do?"

As the passenger train began pulling slowly out of the station, Oliver did the only thing he knew how to do. Instinctively, he ran along the prairie side of the train. Reaching up for two railings that ran along the sides of the passenger train doors, he hoisted himself aboard. With a place to rest his feet, and a rail to wrap his arm through, Oliver found renewed strength.

"I reckon I can ride this way at least until dark," he reasoned.

As the passenger train whizzed along at forty miles an hour, the cooling air of evening slapped hard at Oliver's face, keeping him awake. He followed the same routine of jumping off and hiding in the grass each time the passenger train slowed to stop at a town, exchanging travelers. As night fell and only the faintest bit of evening light shown in the Kansas sky, Oliver saw a wide turn in the track ahead. As the train sped along through the turn, he closed his eyes and mouthed a silent prayer.

"Please God, don't let that conductor look out a window now," he begged. "He'll spot me hangin' onto this door for sure."

Just as Oliver opened his eyes, he saw the conductor's head emerge from the window of the first car behind the engine.

"I'm caught, oh geez, I'm in trouble now!" Oliver said in a panic.

Within a minute, the conductor had traveled through the passenger cars reaching the car onto which Oliver clung for dear life. Unlatching the door and sliding it open just enough to reach out, he grabbed Oliver and yanked him onto the train.

"What in the blazes do you think you're doing?" the conductor scolded him. Kicking Oliver in the seat of the pants, he pushed him towards the back of the train. "Are you trying to get yourself killed or something?"

The conductor pushed and shoved Oliver through several cars until they reached the last car of the passenger train – the smoking car. This was the only car in which passengers were permitted to smoke and it was dark and smelled badly. Putting Oliver in the last seat, the conductor left for the front of the train, mumbling as he went.

Finally able to sit, Oliver realized just how exhausted he had become. As he curled up in the seat with his head resting against the window, he drifted off to sleep. His last conscious thought was that he should probably thank God for not answering his prayer. He needed to be found.

* * * *

"Come on, Sonny. You'll have to get off here now," the conductor said as he nudged Oliver from a deep sleep.

As he rubbed his eyes and sat up in his seat, Oliver took a few seconds to remember where he was. The morning sun shone brightly through the train windows. Squinting, he looked around slowly as the events of the previous day came back to him.

"Did I sleep here all night?" Oliver wanted to know.

"That you did. Now get yourself up and off this train. We're changing engines and then we'll be pulling out," the conductor told Oliver, "and stay away from these passenger trains. There's a freight train pulling out right after we leave. Get on that, and be careful. You look awful young to be riding these trains by yourself."

Oliver took the conductor's advice and headed towards the freight train. He was groggy and disoriented and his stomach was beginning to ache from emptiness.

"Gosh," Oliver thought, "they let me ride that passenger train till the sun came up. I guess they felt sorry for me."

Walking towards the freight train in the distance, Oliver glanced up at a sign post nailed to the platform. It read, COLBY, KANSAS. Just underneath was a second sign that said, GOODLAND – 45 MILES.

"Goodland... why that's only about thirty miles from Colorado," Oliver said out loud to no one. "I must've rode those trains nearly two hundred miles!"

Oliver ran around behind the passenger train and headed for the back of the freight train. Before he could reach it, the freight train slowly began pulling away. Oliver knew he had to be on that train, so he started running just as fast as he could. Reaching an open boxcar door, he was startled to see ten to fifteen hobos inside. Two of them reached out and grabbed Oliver by the shoulders, yanking him into the car.

"Thank you kindly," Oliver said, as he looked the situation over.

"You headed to the harvest fields for work?" one hobo asked.

Oliver thought for just a moment. It sounded like a good idea to him. "Yep," he replied, "that's just where I'm headed."

* * * *

As the hobos settled into the loose straw that lined the boxcar floor, Oliver took a seat in the doorway where he allowed his legs to swing over the side. A quiet peace settled over him as he looked out at the passing prairie.

Hobo hopping into boxcar... just as Oliver did

"What a beautiful country," he thought to himself. Oliver's mind wandered back to his first train ride so many years ago. He remembered the feelings of excitement that he and Edward shared as they anticipated the many adventures that were to come. He also remembered the pact that the brothers had made to stay together, no matter what. He thought of Edward, as he had so many times since that fateful day in Mankato. Where was he? What had happened to the promise that the farmers had made to the boys?

"Some promises just shouldn't be made," Oliver said quietly. "I never should've let those two farmers talk us into bein' split up. I'll never forgive them that lie." The bitterness he felt towards farmer McCammon and farmer Gish was still a fresh taste in Oliver's mouth. He silently vowed to find his younger brother, no matter what the cost.

Oliver shifted in the boxcar doorway. As he did, he felt the barrel of his .22 revolver in the pocket of his overalls. He took it out and looked it over, realizing that it was his one true possession. As the train chugged along, Oliver started taking shots at passing cottonwood trees and fence posts. He had hit three in a row when one of the hobos noticed what he was doing.

"You crazy fool! You better get rid of that thing. Throw it away! Throw it out in the grass," the hobo shouted in alarm at Oliver. "You get caught with that thing and it's thirty days in jail!"

Oliver had no idea he could go to jail for carrying his gun on a train. He surely was not going to throw it away, but he did slip it back into his pocket. Having been to jail three times already in his young life, he had no intention of ever going there again – especially not an adult jail.

"The rules," Oliver said quietly, "you gotta follow the rules. That's the answer to stayin' out of jail and out of trouble in this world. I've learned me that lesson, that's for sure."

CHAPTER THIRTEEN
Oliver's Dream

As the heat of the afternoon sun began making the boxcar unbearable, the freight train's whistle sounded their arrival in Goodland, Kansas, just east of the Colorado line.

"Now listen up," one hobo began. "We're not workin' for a penny less than four dollars and fifty cents a day, plus board. We gotta all stick to that. If none of us is gonna work for less, them farmers will have to pay what we're askin'. Is everyone in on that?"

Everyone nodded their agreement as the train came to a stop. The hobos, with Oliver among them, climbed out of the boxcar. They found a grassy spot to rest as they waited for the farmers to come into town. This was the heart of the wheat belt and there was plenty of work to be had harvesting the fields.

Oliver laid down on his back chewing a piece of the tall grass. He watched as several black crows circled above him. The heat of the day, coupled with the mesmerizing circling of the crows overhead, made Oliver feel groggy. He slowly drifted off to sleep.

As Oliver entered a deep sleep, he began to hear the voices of a dream as he found himself back on Frank McCammon's farm.

"Hey, Oliver!" called out his friend Guy Ball. "Check out all the nests over in these trees. I claim this section of the crick!"

Running over to where Guy stood, Oliver raised his head, watching as the sky blackened with thousands of migrating crows.

Oliver and his friends, Guy and Cliff, had been in town when it was announced that a bounty had been placed on crows. The numbers had gotten out of control and they were feeding on the farmer's crops, threatening to destroy the harvest.

"Five cents a head," Oliver shouted over to Cliff. "We're gonna get rich off of these birds! I claim this section next to Guy."

All three boys staked out their claims along the crick and then settled in to wait as the crows returned to their nests for the evening.

As night fell, the men from the town made their way to the crick carrying their pump guns. Aiming their guns towards the tree tops, they began shooting. The noise was near deafening. The guns popped and the crows squawked as they fell like rain from their perches.

Oliver, Guy, and Cliff ran around under the trees where the crows lay scattered about. With their hunting knives drawn, they quickly chopped off the heads, stashing them into their leather pouches, which were slung over their shoulders. They had to work fast.

As the shooting subsided, the boys could hear the angry shouts of the townsmen. "Get away from those crows!" the voices called in Oliver's direction, as the boys ran from the crick.

Once they were at a safe distance, the three friends sat down to examine their pouches.

"Not bad," Cliff suggested, "not bad at all, I'd say."

"Yeah," replied Oliver, "but I got another idea how we can collect even more."

"A legal way?" Guy wanted to know.

"Of course it's legal," answered Oliver. "You won't find me breakin' the law and goin' to jail. No sir, this is perfectly legal."

"Let's hear it then," Guy said.

"Here's what we do," began Oliver. "We come back in the morning see, when the adult crows are out of the nests huntin' for food. We climb up the trees and get the hatchlings before they can fly. Who knows how much we'll be able to add to our catch – probably hundreds!"

"Not bad, not bad at all!" Cliff smiled as he spoke.

Guy agreed. "We'll meet back here first thing in the morning."

At the crack of dawn, the three friends met up again at the crick and put their plan into motion. Oliver had brought along some boxes and a sack of salt.

"What are they for?" asked Guy.

"I don't feel right about just leavin' the bodies here on the ground," started Oliver. "I'm gonna put 'em in these boxes and cover 'em up with salt to keep 'em from rottin', then I'm gonna bury 'em."

"You're too soft, Oliver," replied Cliff. "The bodies will just be food for some other animals. Don't go to all that trouble."

"I'm buryin' the bodies just the same," Oliver shrugged. "It's bad enough we gotta kill these crows, the least we can do is bury 'em."

"Suit yourself," Guy said. "Now let's get to work."

The three boys climbed tree after tree gathering baby crows. It didn't take long before their leather pouches were full. As his friends ran off to collect their bounty, Oliver stayed back to salt and bury the bodies of the hatchlings. Once finished, he too headed off to town, excited to see how much money he had made.

* * * *

Oliver woke from his dream to find a farmer kicking at his foot. "You lookin' for a job, boy?" the farmer asked.

"Yes sir, I am," replied Oliver, looking up hopefully at the farmer. "How much do you pay?"

"We're payin' four dollars a day and board," the farmer answered firmly.

Oliver remembered what he and the hobos had agreed to on the boxcar. "No, I won't go out for that. I want four and a half a day."

"Well, okay, suit yourself," shrugged the farmer. "If you change your mind, I'll be down there in the Implement Shop."

Oliver got to thinking. "Geez," he said to himself, as he remembered his dream, "I had me close to thirty dollars in the bank back in Esbon from those crows. Why didn't I think of that before I ran off? Now I got only a few cents in my pocket and I ain't eaten all day."

Oliver rose to his feet and headed off towards the Implement Shop. There wasn't much to think about after all. He needed to eat. He knew if he ran out of money he'd have to do something, and he wasn't going to be stealing or anything like that. He hoped that the hobos wouldn't think poorly of him, but he had to do what he had to do.

"I gotta look out for myself," Oliver mumbled. "No one's lookin' out for me, except me."

Entering the Implement Shop, Oliver looked around and found the farmer who had offered him work. He approached the man saying, "I'll go out with ya for four dollars a day and board."

"Four dollars it is," the farmer answered. "Name's McColl. Burt McColl."

"Oliver Nordmark," Oliver introduced himself, extending his right hand.

CHAPTER FOURTEEN

A Real Workin' Man

"So what brings you to these parts, Oliver?" Burt McColl asked, as he loaded up his wagon with the tools he had purchased from the Implement Shop.

Oliver hadn't had much time to think about that one. What *had* brought him to Goodland, Kansas? The only thing he knew for sure was that he wanted to get away from McCammon's farm in Esbon and start a life of his own. Most of all, he wanted to find his brother, Edward. Before he could do any of that, he needed to get some money in his pockets and food in his belly.

"Just lookin' for work," Oliver replied, as he pitched in to help McColl finish loading the wagon.

"Well, I got plenty of that to keep you busy," answered McColl as he stopped to wipe the sweat from his brow. "Wheat fields as far as your eye can see, and all of it needin' to be harvested by fall."

"I reckon I'm up to the task," said Oliver as he mentally added up the money he could expect to make in the next month or two.

"Have you finished your schooling?" McColl asked, as he tried to size up the young man he had just hired.

"Finished eighth grade," Oliver said proudly. "Even earned a gold star for attendance, so I figure I was there for everything they thought I needed to know."

"Hop on in the wagon then." McColl smiled as he motioned to Oliver. "We'd better get started. It'll be a twenty mile ride northwest out to my farm, and I don't much like ridin' after nightfall."

Oliver settled into the back of the wagon as Burt McColl climbed onto the wagon's flat bench seat. Making a clicking sound from the side of his mouth, the farmer shook the reins, encouraging the horse forward. As they pulled away from the small town of Goodland, Oliver felt a sense of light-hearted freedom.

"I'm on my way," he thought. "Nothin' ventured, nothin' gained – and I plan on gainin'."

* * * *

The ride to Burt McColl's farm was a long one. They passed several other small farms along the way which had peculiar looking buildings. Oliver wanted to ask about them, but didn't want to seem stupid. Finally, his curiosity got the better of him.

"What are all them dirt buildings for?" Oliver asked Burt McColl.

"Dirt buildings?" McColl questioned. "You mean the sod houses?"

"Is that what ya call 'em?" Oliver asked.

"Most all the buildings out here are made of sod," began McColl. "We call 'em soddies for short – houses, outbuildings, even barns. In fact,

I'm the only farmer out in these parts that has a frame barn. Sod's the building material of choice out here on the prairie. There's plenty of it and free of charge – no need to be haulin' expensive lumber all the way out from town."

"Makes sense to me," replied Oliver.

This was all new to Oliver, so he decided to end the conversation before he made an even bigger fool of himself. Sitting quietly, he wondered just how these farmers managed to turn dirt from the earth into buildings large enough to live in. What a lot of work that must be. What kind of tools must they need to get that job done?

"Now this here's the start of my land," Burt McColl said, as he broke into Oliver's train of thought. "My daddy bought this land for a dollar an acre – as far as your eye can see."

Oliver stretched his neck in all directions wondering just how many acres McColl must have.

"I've got four brothers and one sister. You got any brothers, Oliver?" Burt McColl wanted to know.

Oliver looked across the wheat fields with a searching, faraway look in his eyes. He did have a brother. Edward was somewhere out there but Oliver didn't know where. He really didn't want to get into all that with Burt McColl, at least not yet.

"Yeah, I got me a brother, but he's back in Esbon," Oliver lied. "He's younger than me."

"Well, my youngest brother is about your age," McColl told Oliver. "You'll be mostly workin' with him. His name's Walter, but we all call him Walt.

"Sounds good to me," Oliver replied as he gazed out across the wheat field. "That sounds good to me."

* * * *

At his first dinner in the home of Burt McColl, Oliver learned all about the way in which wheat is grown as well as the type of work he would be doing bringing in the harvest.

"Now there's a number of operations involved in the production of wheat," Burt McColl began in an authoritative voice. "It all begins with preparing and tilling the soil. Next, we plant the seed and help the crop grow. Come harvest time, which is where we are now, we start with cutting off the ripe plants. Next, we bind the wheat stalks into sheaves and then stack the sheaves into shocks in the fields. When all that's done, we'll begin bringing the sheaves into the barn for threshing."

"Threshing?" Oliver questioned.

"That's where we separate out the grain to be sent to the mill for grinding," replied McColl, as his younger brother, Walt, snickered at Oliver's lack of knowledge.

Oliver bit his tongue. He didn't want to lose this job before it even got started.

"We'll be starting at the crack of dawn," McColl warned, "so I suggest we all get a good night's sleep. It'll be some long days from here on out."

* * * *

Even before the dawn, Oliver awoke to the sound of a rooster crowing. He had been given a place in the loft of the barn to sleep and store his few possessions. He had carefully hidden his .22 revolver deep in the hay and used the blanket that Mrs. McColl had left for him to cover the spot, making a comfortable bed. He had slept soundly and found himself wide awake and eager to start earning his wage as a real workin' man.

"No more free labor from Oliver Nordmark," Oliver said to himself. "Anyone wants a day's work from me, they'll have to pay for it from now on. And I'll give 'em a good day's work no matter what they put me to, but now I'm doin' it for me."

Oliver hopped up and washed his face in the water trough then headed for the house. After a filling, hot breakfast with the McColl family, the men headed out to the barn.

"Now this here's the reaper," began Burt McColl, who never tired of talking farming – especially when it came to machinery and the latest type of equipment. "Cuttin' the grain used to require the use of sickles and cradle-scythes, but not anymore. All that stoopin' and bendin' for acre upon acre is a thing of the past. With this reaper, I just hitch up two of my best horses and lead them along through the fields. See this cuttin' bar?"

Oliver bent down to look at the underside of the reaper where McColl was directing his gaze.

"Now all those knives on the cuttin' bar," continued Burt, "are powered by this wheel on the machine. That bar will cut off the wheat stalks real close to the ground."

"What do me and Walt do?" Oliver asked, eager to get started.

"I'm getting to that," McColl replied. "After the stalks are cut, they fall onto this wooden deck and are swept off onto the ground in a continuous path. You two will rake the stalks into bundles – we call them sheaves – about as big around as your arms can reach, then tie them up with twine. Once you have six sheaves, you stand them up and lean them against each other with the heads up – that's called a shock. Any questions?"

Shocking and binding wheat on Burt McColl's Farm

"Yeah, I got a question," Walt spoke with his head cocked to one side and his hands in his pockets. "Is it quittin' time yet?"

"Very funny," his older brother flatly responded. "Let's get to work."

* * * *

They all left the barn and headed for the fields. Oliver quickly learned the skill of gathering the stalks into sheaves, binding them with twine, and stacking them skyward in groups of six. The work proved to be grueling as the morning wore on. The heat of the sun beat down and the tedious task of raking and tying began to cause his arms and hands to ache. Oliver was used to hard work though, and he kept up his pace right through until lunchtime. Walt, on the other hand, was over twenty yards back from Oliver and falling further behind. Oliver could tell that this youngest of the McColl brothers was a lazy sort, obviously not wanting to do any more than he had to. Burt McColl pulled his horses and the reaper to a stop. Climbing down off his seat, he walked back towards Oliver, motioning Walt to run up and meet him.

"What in the dickins is going on here, you lazy cuss," McColl shouted his disapproval at his youngest brother. "Look at this kid," he pointed at Oliver. "Half your size and doing more than a man's work! And you – you're doing hardly nothing compared to him." Grabbing Oliver's hand, Burt McColl continued, "Look at these hands. Rough as leather with the calluses of a man who knows the meaning of a day's work. You could learn a thing or two from someone who knows how to work like that, Walt."

Shaking his head in disgust, Burt McColl unhitched the horses and headed towards the farmhouse for the afternoon meal. Walt also headed for the house, but Oliver just stood there in the middle of the wheat field, unable to move. He felt ashamed as he repeated Burt McColl's words over and over in his head. This was a new experience for him. Having his work ethic compared to Walt's for the purpose of making Walt feel bad – even worthless – left Oliver feeling bad himself. Should he slow down and keep pace with Walt? Should he keep working hard and hope that Walt would start working harder too? He didn't want to be fired. He needed this job if he was ever going to have enough money to start looking for Edward. He had hoped to become friends with Walt, but slowly he began to realize that he would need to make a choice. Oliver knew that he would always choose Edward, so working hard was the answer. Friendship was going to have to wait.

CHAPTER FIFTEEN

Oliver's New Job

Oliver worked for Burt McColl during the harvest of 1913. He quickly became skilled at all aspects of bringing in the wheat crop and earned one hundred and fifty-six dollars for himself in the process. As August came to a close and the work was finishing up, Oliver knew that he would soon be moving on. Another opportunity, however, was about to present itself. As he worked one Saturday afternoon at cleaning up the harvesting equipment, Oliver was approached by Burt McColl's brother, John, with an offer.

"Well Oliver, my brother tells me you were a great help bringing in the wheat crop," John McColl said as he stood with arms crossed over his chest. "Now that the harvest is all but complete, what are your plans?"

"No set plans really," Oliver replied. "I guess I'll be headin' back to Goodland, then maybe ride east a bit."

"What about workin' for me?" John suggested. "I've got some land north of here that I need to put a house on before my wife will head up there with me."

"I don't know nothin' about buildin' houses," Oliver said in a puzzled voice. "I don't know how much help I would be for that."

"Well, it seems you didn't know much about harvesting either, and you did alright there," John complimented him. "I plan to build a sod house, which I've done before, so what I need is a hard worker to help me with the lifting. Now I can't be paying the same as my brother, but I can offer you thirty dollars a month and board. What do you say?" John McColl asked hopefully.

Now of course Oliver had stretched the truth a bit when he told John that he had plans to head back to Goodland. He really had no plan at all, and certainly there was nothing in Goodland for him. A few more months of work would bring his savings up well over two hundred dollars. He would need all of that and maybe more to start his search for Edward. Burt McColl had been a good man to work for and although Oliver had only met John a few times since he had been there, he hoped that the two brothers were cut from the same cloth.

"Okay, I'll go out with you," Oliver decided.

"Great!" John replied with a sigh of relief. "We'll head out the first of the month. I'm sure Burt will let you stay here in the loft until then. I'll go and run it by him."

The two shook hands and John headed out of the barn towards his brother's house. Oliver got back to the task of cleaning the reaper, feeling very lucky that his future was settled – at least for the next few months.

* * * *

The first of September was a dreary, rainy day with a light fog settling on the prairie. John McColl arrived bright and early in his horse-drawn wagon loaded with all sorts of supplies. There were building materials and tools, canvas tarps and poles to build a temporary shelter, cooking supplies and more. Oliver noticed a large sled-like object and wondered to himself why they would need a sled. He decided to wait and find out, rather than ask questions just yet.

Bidding farewell to Burt McColl and his family, Oliver loaded his few possessions into the wagon, and the two of them headed off across the prairie. It was nearly a six hour ride before the sight of a large windmill came into view.

"Home sweet home!" John McColl shouted with a big grin on his face.

Oliver was puzzled. "Are we here?" he wondered out loud.

"Yes indeed," said John. "So far it's just a windmill that pumps water from the well I dug, but with a little hard work it'll be a real home in no time."

Oliver remembered back to his wagon ride from Goodland to Burt McColl's farm when he had seen a sod house for the first time. He had marveled at the thought of making a house fit to live in from the very earth beneath his foot. He could feel the excitement inside him as he realized that he was about to learn how to do just that.

Pulling the wagon near the windmill, John McColl jumped from the wagon and began unloading things from the back.

"We'll set up our tent here against the side of the wagon and rest up tonight," John spoke as he continued unloading. "Tomorrow we'll get started on building the house."

Oliver, who felt no need to rest up, tried to hide his disappointment at having to wait another day to get started. He pitched in to help unload the wagon, then he and John erected the shelter. They enjoyed a light supper before turning in for the night.

* * * *

Oliver awoke just as the morning sun rose in the eastern sky. He gazed across the prairie at the bright yellow sunflowers that dotted his view for as far as his eye could see. John stirred under the canvas shelter, stretched his arms and woke to greet the day.

"What a beautiful morning," John spoke in a hushed tone.

The rays of morning sunshine danced along the tips of the dew-covered grasses, creating beautiful prisms of light and color. Both John McColl and Oliver sat quietly for a long moment taking in the beauty before them.

"A perfect day to build a house," Oliver spoke, breaking the silence.

"A perfect day it is," John agreed. "What do you say we have some breakfast and head out to find just the right place to start cuttin' sod?"

"I'm ready for that!" Oliver smiled.

* * * *

Building a house of sod turned out to be very hard work. The first thing that needed to be done was to find a large level area of prairie where the grass was real thick. Thick grasses would mean a dense, continuous mat of roots that would serve to strengthen the bricks of sod. Using long handled sickles, the grasses were then cut down low to the ground and hauled off. Oliver and John worked in half acre parcels. By the end of the first week, they had cleared off several acres of prairie grass, which would produce enough sod to make a small house.

Next came the task of cutting the earth into the shape of bricks. On the morning of the sixth day, John McColl hitched up his horses to the large sled that Oliver had noticed in the back of the wagon.

"Now you see this sled?" John began in explanation as he turned the sled on its side. "These knives stickin' down on each end of the underside are going to cut down deep into the ground. Once we get the whole area cut side to side, then we'll cut the other way – up and down. That'll leave the ground cut in the shape of bricks, you see?"

Oliver marveled at the ingenuity of this process. "What do *we* do while the horses are pulling the sled?"

"We get the easy part," McColl said with a smile. "We sit on the sled to weigh it down so that the knives will dig deep and stay deep. I'll take the reins in the front, and you sit towards the back."

The two workers headed out to begin cutting their bricks of earth. This time they decided to work in more manageable, quarter acre parcels. The bricks were cut in twelve inch strips about four inches thick. Changing direction, the sled next cut the strips into lengths of about three feet long. Finally, a special plow was used that pulled the sod up and flipped it over while keeping the bricks neatly intact.

Oliver and John traveled back to the windmill where they removed the bed from the wagon, replacing it with planks of board. This enabled them to load the heavy bricks of sod more easily onto the flat surface, bringing them back to the windmill where a site was chosen to build the sod house.

"Now the way we lay these sod bricks," John instructed, "is lengthwise, making a wall about two feet thick. Every few layers we reverse the process and lay crosswise to bind the walls and make them solid."

"Grass side up or down?" Oliver asked.

"Always grass side down," replied John, "root side up."

Working day after day laying sod in the same fashion a bricklayer would lay bricks, it took nearly a month to raise the walls of the small sod house. A wooden door frame was set in place on the south side of the house and there were wooden frames where two glass windows would eventually be placed. Since the walls of the house were two feet thick, deep cozy seats were created at each window which would become a favorite spot for Oliver to sit and gaze out across the prairie.

Sod house like the one Oliver built with John McColl

As the construction of the little sod house walls neared completion, Oliver looked skyward and began to wonder.

"How are we gonna put a roof on this house?" he asked John.

"Now that gets a bit tricky," John replied. "First, we'll need to frame out the roof with cottonwood poles, then we'll cover the poles with willow brush and hay. I've got a roll of tar paper that'll go over the hay to try and keep the rain out as much as possible. On top of that, we'll put a thinner layer of sod. If we can get some clay, we'll tamp a layer of that on the very top."

"That sounds like it'll take quite a while to finish," Oliver observed. "We'd better keep workin' to get it done before the weather gets bad."

"Oh, we're going to keep working alright," John spoke as he looked skyward. "I need to get this house done so I can start on a barn for the cattle I plan to bring out here."

"I can help you build the barn too," Oliver offered. "That is if you want me to stay on."

John McColl smiled. "Now I was hoping you might consider that."

Oliver and John grinned at one another, acknowledging that Oliver was doing a good job, and the two of them were enjoying working together. Feeling satisfied with their working arrangements, they put their minds and hands to the task of completing their house of sod.

CHAPTER SIXTEEN
Life in a Sod House

Oliver and John McColl finished building their sod house by the third week of October, 1913. The interior of the small house had two rooms divided by a sod partition. The front door entered into the kitchen where there was a table with four chairs and a stove for cooking. John McColl brought the stove from his father's house in Goodland. The second room was a bedroom with two beds and hooks jammed into the sod walls to hang clothes on. One bed had a curtain attached that could be pulled closed for privacy. This is where John McColl and his wife would sleep. The second, slightly smaller bed, would be for Oliver to share with John's young son, Joseph. The floor of the sod house was dirt, which turned to mud whenever it rained, since the roof had a tendency to leak. Sometimes after a hard rain would end outside, it would continue to 'rain' inside the house for another three or four days. This made it especially hard to keep anything clean. The thick walls of the sod house kept the inside warm in the winter and cool in the summer. During the winter, the family cooked with kerosene, but in the spring, summer, and fall, they would fuel the stove with corncobs or cow chips.

Eva McColl joined her husband in the sod house, along with Joseph, as soon as John and Oliver had it complete and furnished. She had only minor complaints about sod house living and seemed happy with her new home. John was happy to have his family all together again, and he and Oliver began work on a small barn.

Oliver took a liking to young Joseph, for he reminded Oliver of his brother, Edward. He let Joseph tag along when Oliver would take the wagon out on the prairie to collect the cow chips that were used for fuel. Oliver and Joseph would pick up the cow chips, burnt dry from the sun like a pancake, until they had a wagon full. Oliver was surprised at how well the cow chips would burn and without a trace of their original scent.

One night, not long after everyone had fallen asleep, Oliver woke to what felt like biting on his toes. As he sat up, he felt something move, followed by a loud rumbling sound, like a herd of running cattle. He quickly reached for the kerosene lamp.

"Ugh!" Oliver screamed. "Rats, rats! There's rats everywhere!"

Joseph sat up just as John McColl was bringing another lamp into the room. Rats were all over the bed and running across the floor, headed for the holes they had dug into the sod walls.

"Momma, Momma!" cried Joseph in a panic.

Eva quickly removed Joseph from the bed and carried him into the kitchen.

"Sorry 'bout that," Oliver apologized, as he and John shooed the last of the rats from the room. "They just took me by surprise, bitin' on my toes like that."

Winter on the prairie at John McColl's Homestead

"It's okay," John replied. "We'll have to get to work tomorrow filling up all those holes. That'll be a regular task now that colder weather is coming."

"Ah geez," said Oliver in disgust as he looked down at his shoes lying by the bed. "They've been chewin' on my shoes."

"Well that's a lesson for you. You'll want to tie the laces together and hang them from the bedpost so they can't do that again," John advised.

John and Oliver joined Eva and Joseph, who was now wide awake, in the kitchen for a cup of tea as they all calmed down from such an exciting start to the night.

* * * *

Oliver stayed with John McColl and his family through the winter and into the spring of 1914. The time passed quickly since there was always so much to do. They finished the sod barn for the small herd of cattle that John had brought to his homestead. In the spring, they put in a vegetable garden to help feed the family. By early summer, Oliver could feel change in the air.

"Oliver, I need to talk to you," began John McColl as he and Oliver headed out of the barn. "I'm afraid I'm not going to be able to keep you on much longer. We've got another baby on the way, and things will be getting mighty crowded in this small of a house. Not to mention, I'm running out of money to keep paying you."

"I've been thinkin' it's about time for me to be movin' on anyway," Oliver lied. He had become used to living in the sod house and he was genuinely fond of John McColl and his young family. He would be sorry to leave.

"Well then, the timing is right," John continued. "You can stay on for another couple of weeks while you decide what you're going to do."

"Thanks, I appreciate that," replied Oliver as they reached the house. "I'll be movin' on soon."

CHAPTER SEVENTEEN
One More McColl

O n the evening before Oliver was to leave John McColl's home, John's oldest brother, Doc McColl, showed up at the door of the sod house just in time for supper. They all shared a last meal of chicken and potatoes, talking lightheartedly about their past year together.

"Yeah, I wasn't so sure what I'd got myself into," Oliver said with a snicker. "I never knew nothin' about building a house of sod, but the money sure sounded good."

"Oh, I knew you'd be a big help getting the house built," replied John. "My only worry was whether or not you'd stay on, after that episode with the rats!"

"I hate rats," little Joseph piped in. "Oliver has to fill the holes so the rats won't eat me in the night."

"I'm afraid I won't be fillin' no more rat holes, Joseph." Oliver smiled at the boy. "Your papa's gonna have to take over that job. I'm gonna be movin' on in the morning."

Joseph looked sadly towards Oliver, as tears welled in the corners of his eyes. His mother had explained to him that Oliver would be leaving soon, but that didn't change the fact that Joseph would surely miss his only friend, whom he had come to look upon as a big brother.

"It's okay, Joseph. You're a big boy now so your papa's gonna need your help around here," Oliver said, coaxing a smile from the five-year-old.

Oliver wanted to say that the two of them would see each other again, but he was hesitant to make a promise that he might not be able to keep. He would always remember the promise he had made to Edward. The promise to stay together was one that Oliver just couldn't keep. He knew now that it hadn't been his fault, but he felt responsible nonetheless for the heartbreak that had followed. No, he wouldn't make any promises to Joseph. Oliver was good at learning life's lessons.

"Where ya headed?" Doc McColl asked as he broke into Oliver's thoughts.

"I guess I'll catch a train out of Goodland and head back towards Esbon to look for some work," Oliver replied. "Somethin' might come up along the way."

"How about something right in Goodland?" suggested Doc. "My place is about fifteen miles outside of town, and I could use a good pair of hands. I can pay you same as John here – thirty dollars a month and board. What do ya say?"

"I say you got yourself a hired hand!" said Oliver, with a satisfied grin.

* * * *

Oliver headed off to Goodland with Doc McColl the following morning. As he waved good-bye to John McColl, his wife, and young son,

Oliver thought reflectively on his time in the sod house. He had managed to bring his savings from one hundred and fifty-six dollars to three hundred and seventy-two dollars. He had needed to spend some of his earnings on a winter coat and a new pair of boots. He had two pair of overalls and two shirts now, and he had also purchased socks and underwear. He figured he would work for Doc McColl for a while and hope to bring his savings up to five hundred dollars. Once he had that much, he would have enough to start his search for Edward.

Oliver Nordmark – Age 16

"What kind of crops you puttin' in, Mr. McColl?" asked Oliver, breaking the silence.

"First of all, you need to call me Doc," began his new boss. "Everyone calls me Doc, even my own children. I can't think of anyone who calls me Mr. McColl, so there's no reason for you to start." He smiled in Oliver's direction then continued. "I'll be puttin' in wheat, barley and oats. After all the crops are in, we'll be startin' work on a frame house – one of the first in the area. I've got a sod house now. It's a real nice one but my family's growing and I think it's time to move up to a frame house. So, if you're up for it after the crops are in, you can stay on and help with that."

"I'm up for it," Oliver said with a smile. "I'll be lookin' forward to learnin' how to do that."

* * * *

Oliver settled in at Doc McColl's place and worked the planting season. It was hard work but nothing Oliver wasn't used to. Doc's plans to get started on a new frame house that winter had to be put on hold when he came down with severe stomach pains. After a trip to the local doctor in Goodland, he was rushed to Kansas City for an operation to have his appendix removed.

It was up to Oliver to see that all the work got done on the farm while Doc was gone. Since the crops were in, this meant taking care of the cattle and other animals.

One stormy winter day, as Oliver tried to pump water for the cattle, the little gasoline engine that powered the pump started missing and backfiring. He had learned a thing or two about gas engines over the course of the last year and a half, so he started to tinker with it. He wore a hand-me-down pair of mittens with ragged edges, and his fingers were just about numb from the freezing cold. Just as Oliver pushed down on the governor to make it go faster, his stringy mitten got caught in the gears. Before he knew what had happened, the gears had taken the end of his thumb off!

Numbed by the cold and shocked at seeing the tip of his thumb missing and blood everywhere, Oliver tried to stay calm and take control of the situation. He rushed to the telephone and quickly called Doc McColl's brother, Burt, who lived a few miles away.

"Burt McColl?" Oliver asked in a panic. "It's me, Oliver Nordmark, over at your brother Doc's place. I tore my finger off in the pump engine. It's torn clean off and bleeding everywhere!"

"Calm down, Oliver," an anxious Burt replied. "I'm on my way. Wrap it in a clean rag till I get there."

The phone line went dead. Oliver looked around for the cleanest rag he could find, squeezing it on the top of his thumb.

When Burt McColl arrived in his jalopy Ford, he helped Oliver inside and quickly drove off to the nearest doctor, who was about fifteen miles away.

"This storm's a bad one," observed Burt. "You hold on tight and keep the pressure on that thumb."

"I will," shivered Oliver, "but it's pulsing with pain!"

Freezing rain and ice poured down on the old jalopy, making it harder and harder for Burt McColl to see where they were going. Without warning, the steering gave way and Burt suddenly lost all control. The car veered to the right and took on a mind of its own, sliding around on the ice. Finally coming to a stop, Burt tried to steer the old Ford back onto the road. The tires couldn't get traction, spinning wildly in place. Burt finally let up off the gas.

"We're stuck," he said somberly. "You'll have to get out and help me push to get off this ice."

Oliver glanced down at his aching, torn thumb. He tried his best to tuck his hand up into his coat sleeve, pulled his collar up around his neck, and opened his door. The freezing rain was coming down in sheets that seemed to instantly drench him the moment he stepped out of the car. As Oliver ran around to the back, Burt opened his window and yelled to him.

"On the count of three, now... One... Two... Three!"

Oliver pushed with all the weight of his shoulders, trying to protect his injured thumb. The old Ford struggled on the ice, spewing exhaust in Oliver's face and kicking up ice and water. Finally, it lurched forward.

"Get in, we're moving!" yelled Burt from the driver's seat.

Oliver ran to jump in the passenger side, as the door flung in the wind. Reaching to slam the door shut, he felt the wooziness of unconsciousness creep over him, as he passed out from exhaustion and pain.

* * * *

Spring seemed to arrive overnight in Goodland, Kansas that winter of 1915. Doc McColl had recovered from his surgery, and Oliver had survived the loss of his thumb tip. Burt McColl had managed to get the unconscious teenager to Dr. Heald's office in Goodland where he was revived with smelling salts. The doctor then proceeded to trim off the wound with a pair of scissors, apply an antiseptic salve and wrap it tightly closed. With time, he told Oliver, the skin would grow together, sealing off the wound.

It was mid-April when Doc McColl approached Oliver about the frame house.

"I'm going to get started on my new house," Doc informed Oliver. "If you're still interested, I could use the help. If not, you'll have to be leaving."

"Oh, I'm still interested," Oliver replied. "Half a thumb's not gonna slow me down."

"Now I was hoping you'd feel that way," Doc said. "The first of the lumber's scheduled to be delivered by the end of the week."

"End of the week it is then!" Oliver replied.

* * * *

Oliver soon learned that building a frame house required a lot of skill. He didn't have much experience with a hammer, and working with a missing thumb tip made handling tools a bit more difficult. He often missed the nail he was trying to drive into the wood, hitting his left hand instead. He figured he bent and ruined nearly as many nails as those he successfully drove through the boards. He was frustrated and discouraged. To make matters worse, Doc McColl's son, eight-year-old Willie, was a devil of a kid who took pleasure out of tormenting Oliver at every opportunity. Doc often witnessed his son's antics, but he never intervened. Oliver was reluctant to speak up or complain about the boy, since he didn't want to risk losing his job before he reached his goal of earning five hundred dollars. Finally though, the taunting got the best of him.

As Oliver worked hammering nails in the heat of the afternoon, Willie approached him carrying a gas lamp that had been hanging on the wall in the sod house kitchen.

"Hey, Oliver," Willie teased as he swung the lamp in front of his face. "Need some more light to see what you're doin'?"

"No, I don't need no lamp in the middle of the day," Oliver said through clenched teeth.

Swinging the lamp again and again, Willie went on. "Are you sure you don't need more light to see them nails?"

"No," Oliver bit his lip, "I'm seeing just fine."

Hearing the exchange between Willie and Oliver, Doc McColl looked over and snickered. Willie was his only son and he was slow to see any wrong in his actions. He was just a boy having fun, as far as Doc was concerned.

Oliver caught Doc's gaze, expecting that he would finally intervene on his behalf. When Doc turned back to his work without a word of reproach towards Willie, Oliver lost his composure.

"That's enough for me," Oliver said in disgust as he threw down his hammer. "I'm quittin'."

No one said a word as Oliver headed towards the sod house muttering to himself and shaking his head. He came back out of the house with his bag of possessions in hand and began walking in the direction of town. Doc McColl said nothing as he looked up from his work to see Oliver walking off.

As the afternoon sun lowered in the sky, Oliver continued on his fifteen mile hike towards Goodland. The more he walked, the less frustrated he became and the more he started looking forward. As he lay under the night sky of the Kansas prairie, Oliver drifted off to sleep with thoughts of Edward.

"I'm finally on my way," he thought. "I don't have quite as much money as I had hoped, but it's enough to get started."

* * * *

Oliver woke at the first hint of daylight. He felt a little tickle on his arm and lifted his head to see what it was. He was surprised to find a little garter snake coiled up right next to him.

"Well, little fellow," he spoke to the snake, "I guess you're all alone and looking for a cozy place to sleep too." Oliver sat up and continued his one-sided conversation with his new acquaintance. "You know, I'm not afraid of any snake – especially a harmless little garter like you – so you don't have to worry 'bout me tryin' to kill you or nothin'. I come up against a rattlesnake once, you know. I was ridin' an old mare, see, and the mare seen the rattler first and froze up stiff. Slow as could be, I got down off that mare, took the rein off, and *snapped* that rattlesnake on the top of his head till he coiled up with his head in the middle. Then I flipped him over, grabbed him, and put him in a sack."

Looking down at the little garter snake, he went on with his story. "Yep, I had me a rattlesnake in a sack. I was just new to workin' at Doc McColl's place and after I took the cows in, I took that sack into the front yard where he was standin'. 'See what I got?' I says to him all innocent like. Then I threw that rattlesnake right out on the ground in front of him – 'bout near gave him a heart attack, I think. Then he says to me, 'Geez, boy! If you do that again, you'll be going down the road!' He was not happy with me!"

Gazing up at the rising sun, Oliver pondered his time with Doc McColl.

"No," he said out loud. "I don't think me and old Doc McColl were meant to be workin' together. We never saw eye to eye on much of anything."

Oliver stood and gathered his belongings, being careful not to disturb the little snake.

"See ya later little garter snake," he said, as he prepared to continue his journey. "Have a nice life, and watch out for rattlers and farmers with devilish kids."

CHAPTER EIGHTEEN
The Search Begins

"I'd like a one way ticket to Esbon, Kansas please," Oliver said to the ticket agent behind the train station window.

"That'll be twelve dollars and sixty-eight cents, young man," the agent replied as he took Oliver's money and handed him a boarding pass. "Train leaves in a little more than an hour."

Oliver looked around and spotted the General Store where he bought himself a sandwich and took it back to the platform, settling in for a bite to eat. He glanced down at his ticket with pride as he remembered all he had accomplished in the last two years. He would spend this train ride seated comfortably on the leather seat of the train car. No more hanging onto the outside of the car trying to stay awake. This time he would arrive at his destination refreshed and well rested. More importantly, this time he actually had a destination. Oliver had decided on his walk to Goodland that he would begin his search by going back to visit Frank McCammon in Esbon. His hope was that McCammon would have some answers as to Edward's whereabouts.

"All aboard!" the train conductor called out.

Oliver rose from the platform and followed the small crowd of waiting passengers onto the train car. He chose a seat about halfway down the aisle and settled in for the ride. Not long after the train had pulled out of the Goodland Station, the conductor made his way through the train cars collecting each passenger's boarding pass. Oliver smiled as he sat straight up and handed over his pass. As the train headed east, miles and miles of passing prairie set Oliver's mind to thinking. What would happen when he showed up at Frank McCammon's farm? He had left so abruptly that 4th of July in 1913... would McCammon even speak to him? What about the pony that Oliver had left in town that day? Oliver tried not to think about that. Instead, he found himself wondering about 'Little Red.'

'Little Red' was the name that Oliver had given to his pet pig. There had been many pigs on McCammon's farm and one day, when Oliver was about twelve years old, a baby pig had managed to get out of its pen. Running through the barn, the piglet found its way under the legs of a milking cow. The cow became startled and stamped the ground with its hind feet, crushing the back legs of the little piglet. Oliver and Frank McCammon had come running when they heard the pained squeals of the baby pig.

"Take her out in the field," McCammon said as he handed the crying animal to Oliver. "Kill it and bury it. There's nothing else to be done."

Looking down at the injured pig in his arms, Oliver knew that those instructions would be difficult for him to follow.

"Can I have her?" he asked hopefully.

"Yes, you can have her," replied McCammon, as he shook his head and watched young Oliver cradle the piglet, "but she'll die anyway."

Oliver remembered the special care he had given 'Little Red', as she came to be called. First, he made small splints and tied them with rags to the young pig's hind legs. With the splints, the piglet could walk slowly around, dragging her legs behind her. Oliver had kept 'Little Red' in a box while he was working, so that she couldn't go very far and get into more trouble. Feeling that it was too dangerous to keep the injured piglet in the pen with her mother and six siblings, Oliver nursed 'Little Red' back to health himself. He fed his new pet milk from a spoon, and spent his free time coaxing her around the farmyard to strengthen her hind legs.

Time went on and 'Little Red' got better, much to Oliver's delight. She grew out of her box, and soon enjoyed tagging along behind her caregiver, much like a pet dog. Wherever Oliver would show up, there would be 'Little Red' waiting for him. If the pig got in the way as Oliver went about his chores, he would give her a gentle shove. 'Little Red' would roll over, get up, and come right back to Oliver's side. When no one was looking, Oliver would pick 'Little Red' up and throw her in the granary, letting her eat until her heart was content. He continued to give her milk all the time, and she grew to be nice and fat.

"Yep, that was one swell pig," Oliver thought, as he rested his head against the train's window and closed his eyes to nap. "I wonder what ever became of her?"

* * * *

On the afternoon of the second day, the conductor announced that the train would soon be pulling into the Esbon Station. Oliver began to gather his things, then looked out the window to see if he would recognize his surroundings. To his surprise, everything looked pretty much the same as he remembered it.

Main Street – Esbon, Kansas – Early 1900's

The whistle sounded as the train pulled into the station. Oliver rose from his seat and followed several other passengers off the train. Standing in the light of day in the center of town, memories of the more than four years he had spent in Esbon came flooding back. He remembered having a lot of fun here with his school friends, and he remembered feeling very alone at times without his brother. But mostly, it all felt like so long ago. Even though it had been just two years, in many ways it seemed like a lifetime had passed.

"Well," Oliver said to himself, "let's get on with it."

Picking up his bag, he began the seven mile walk towards the farm of Frank McCammon, in search of some answers.

* * * *

"Oliver?" Frank McCammon asked with disbelief. "Is that you? Why you're nearly a grown man. Come in, come in!"

Surprised and pleased by McCammon's welcoming smile, Oliver entered the front room of the farmhouse that had once been his home. He took a quick glance around and marveled that everything was just as it had been.

"Are you hungry?" asked McCammon as he headed down the short hall towards the kitchen.

Oliver had not eaten since lunch and he knew it was past supper. The walk from town, he now realized, had made him especially hungry. Before he could even answer, Frank was motioning Oliver to sit at the table while his wife filled a bowl of stew from the stove. They all sat down as Oliver began eating. There was silence at first, but then Frank McCammon spoke.

"That was one bad thing you did," he said, "leavin' that pony there in the livery stable like that."

Oliver looked up from his bowl feeling instantly like a boy again, having his behavior corrected.

"I know it was," Oliver admitted, "but she was safe, and I wanted to catch that train. I just didn't have time to do anything about it."

"Where have you been?" McCammon asked, changing the subject.

"I've been workin' the last two years straight on farms around Goodland. I learned how to harvest wheat and how to build a sod house," Oliver spoke with pride. "I even helped build a frame house."

"I hope you earned a fair wage," McCammon said, seeming impressed with all that Oliver had learned.

"I saved up near four hundred dollars before I bought a train ticket back here to Esbon," Oliver spoke as he removed his money from his pants pocket, placing it on the table in front of him.

"Oliver!" Mrs. McCammon gasped. "You shouldn't be traveling around with all that money in your pocket. You have to be awfully careful – especially in the cities – someone will steal that from you!"

"I gotta keep it somewhere," Oliver smiled naively. "Can't think of a better place than my pocket."

"Well I can," McCammon replied. "Sewn into your underwear is the best place for a travelin' man to keep his money. Mrs. McCammon here will do the sewin' for you. I'd hate to see you lose that hard-earned money to some thief."

"Well, I'd be much obliged," a more sober Oliver replied, realizing that he still had a lot to learn. "I can't be parting with a dime of that money. I figure I'll be needin' all that and maybe more to track down my brother, Edward."

"Edward?" McCammon raised an eyebrow. "Edward's back East. He hasn't been in these parts for, oh I'd say, five years or more."

"Five years?" Oliver was shocked. "Why didn't you tell me? Why was he sent back East?"

"Well, now that's a sad story," began Frank McCammon, "but since you're nearly grown now, I guess it's time you heard it."

Frank McCammon went on to tell a disbelieving Oliver the events that transpired when Oliver had first come to live with the McCammons, and Edward had gone with William Gish.

The farmers had arranged the first visit for the two brothers about six months after their placements. Oliver had traveled south with McCammon and spent the day at the Gish farm. When Frank

McCammon had attempted to schedule a second visit about a year later, William Gish informed him that young Edward had 'not met with his expectations', and he would soon be contacting the Children's Aid Society to have him removed. When Reverend Swan, the agent from the Society, arrived at the Gish farm, he realized immediately what had happened. Edward had been forced to do the work of a grown man. When the young boy's back was injured, William Gish decided that Edward was no longer any use to him and would need to leave. Since the farmers who were looking for orphans were looking for farm help, Reverend Swan realized that Edward would never be chosen again. He had contacted McCammon to see if he would house the young boy, but with a child of his own on the way, McCammon was reluctant to take on another mouth to feed. With no other options, Reverend Swan made the decision to send Edward back East, where hopefully the Children's Aid Society would be able to find him a home.

McCammon's Home - Early 1900's

"So you see," McCammon finished his story, "Edward is back East somewhere. Maybe he's living with a new family or maybe in one of the orphanages, there's no telling."

* * * *

Oliver spent the night with Frank and Hettie McCammon. As he prepared to leave the following morning, Frank knocked on the door to Oliver's room.

"I'm real sorry about your brother," Frank said. "I didn't tell you about it because I knew there was nothing that could be done."

"Well, there's something I can do about it now," Oliver replied with determination.

McCammon turned to leave the room. "You know," he offered, "you still have that money in the town bank from your bounty hunting. It's not a lot, but it's yours."

"Thanks," Oliver said, "I had forgotten about that."

As Frank McCammon left the room, Oliver called to him. "Hey, what ever happened to 'Little Red'?"

"Oh," McCammon replied with a chuckle, "would you believe she grew up and had young ones of her own? Good thing you were too soft to take her out and kill her!"

* * * *

Oliver walked away from the McCammon farm with enough money to get himself to New York City. His savings was sewn safely into his underwear and his belly was full with the warm breakfast that Mrs. McCammon had fixed for him.

"Yeah," he grinned to himself as he walked along, "I did save that little pig's life. I believe old Frank should have offered to pay me for those young pigs!"

As he kicked a small rock along the dusty road, Oliver headed back to town to see about getting a train ticket to the East Coast.

"And let me say right here that only a young and vigorous tramp is able to deck a passenger train, and also, that young and vigorous tramp must have his nerve with him as well."

~ Jack London, Author

CHAPTER NINETEEN

Riding The Rails

E xiting the town bank in Esbon with his twenty-nine dollars and seventy-seven cents in bounty money shoved deep into his pocket, Oliver Nordmark decided to splurge a bit as he walked towards the General Store. Once inside, he looked around until he found a display of pocket watches. He was surprised at the range of prices for the various watches, and finally settled on the least expensive, silver-plated one. He made his purchase, then headed for the train depot to inquire about a ticket to New York City.

"You can't buy a ticket clear through," the ticket agent informed the young man. "You'll have to buy a ticket here to get you to Chicago on the Kansas City Rock Island Railway, then you'll need to buy a second ticket from Chicago to New York City on the Nickle Plate Line. Mind you now, there might be a layover in Chicago before you can catch a train headed out. The whole trip will probably cost you more than forty dollars."

"I've got that much," Oliver replied as he reached into his pocket. "How much for this leg of the journey?"

"Nineteen dollars and twenty cents to ride from here to Chicago," the agent told Oliver, as he looked skeptically at the hayseed before him.

Oliver placed enough money for a ticket to Chicago on the counter, then put the rest back in his pocket. Heading for the platform, he grew more and more excited about the trip ahead. This would be a three day train ride, and he had enough cash in his pocket for the tickets as well as money to eat along the way.

Oliver's trip to Chicago passed uneventfully. He ate and slept on the passenger train and enjoyed the scenery as he gazed out the window. Upon his arrival at the depot in Chicago, he learned that he would not be able to catch a train to New York City until the following morning. Since he had not budgeted for a hotel room, and he didn't wish to open up the stitching on his underwear to draw from his savings, he decided that he would find a spot near the platform and sleep outside for the night. Oliver walked around Chicago's streets marveling at the sights of the big city and stretching his legs before facing another long train ride in the morning. As night fell, he found a spot on the far side of the train tracks, just out of sight from the depot, and settled down to sleep. His travel bag made a nice pillow, and Oliver had no trouble nodding off.

Waking at the first hint of dawn, Oliver sat up and stretched, rubbed his eyes, and looked around. "I suppose I'll look for a quick bite to eat before boarding the train," he thought.

As he entered a local coffee shop, Oliver reached into his pocket for some money. He felt nothing. In disbelief, he jabbed his hands deep into all his pockets. The only thing he came up with was a few coins from a pocket of his overalls and his watch, which he had tucked away inside his shirt pocket.

"What?" he mumbled to himself. "Where's my... where's my money?"

Slowly Oliver faced the realization that his money was gone. Thinking perhaps that it had fallen out of his pocket while he was sleeping, he ran back to the tree where he had spent the night. Pushing the tall prairie grasses side to side, he frantically searched the area but found nothing. He ripped through his bag of belongings, hoping beyond hope, even though he couldn't remember putting his money in the bag.

After fruitless searching, young Oliver leaned against the tree in despair and slowly slid down the trunk until he was seated on his haunches. He hid his face in his hands as he held back the anger that was raging inside him.

He wasn't sure how much time had passed as he pondered this turn of events, but eventually he lifted his head as he heard a low whistle and looked towards the incoming passenger train. Oliver had planned to purchase his ticket from Chicago to New York City this morning, but now his money was gone and the train would be boarding shortly.

"Some hobo must've stole my money while I was sleeping," Oliver reasoned to himself. "I got no time to unstitch my underwear to use some of my savings. Besides, I'm gonna need that money once I get to New York to live on till I find some kind of work."

As Oliver tried to figure out what to do, darkening storm clouds overhead opened up, and a steady rain began to pour. Looking over at the passenger train, Oliver thought and thought until he came up with an idea. He knew that the water tank behind the passenger train's engine had a flat, square grading on top. He remembered hearing the hobos talk about hitching a ride that way. They called it "decking." If he could get up there unnoticed, he could hold onto the sides and ride to New York that way.

"I'll give it a try," Oliver decided.

As the passengers and railroad employees busied themselves at the depot, Oliver ran about a hundred yards ahead of the station through the tall grass. When no one was looking, he stepped out onto the center of the tracks. He began walking towards the train, making no effort to try to hide himself, looking just like any other working man headed into town. He had timed the train's departure and as he looked down at his watch, he paced himself just right. The moment that the engine's whistle blew and the train inched forward, Oliver climbed up onto the top of the water tank just as he had planned.

"Aw, Geez!" Oliver sighed as he reached the top, only to find that this tank's grading was round, not square. "This is gonna be harder than I thought. I wasn't expectin' this."

Nevertheless, Oliver laid down on the top of the water tank with his bag slung over his neck and held on tight, hoping no one would see him. As the final whistle blew, announcing the train's imminent departure, he looked up and made eye contact with a couple of fellows standing along the road. They started running towards the train and Oliver knew that he had been caught.

"God help me," he mumbled as he gathered his courage, closed his eyes, and jumped from the top of the water tank all the way to the ground below.

Surprised to find himself unhurt, Oliver quickly ran down along the side of the train trying to decide what to do. As a big cloud of steam spewed from the train's engine, he searched for something to grab onto along the side of the train. Finding nothing, he realized that he had no place to go but under the train. Bending down, Oliver saw a three inch wide beam running the length of the train car. There were two smaller round pipes on either side. Experienced in making quick decisions, Oliver did just that. He crawled up onto the main beam on his belly and grabbed the smaller pipes for balance. It briefly crossed his mind that these one inch pipes might well be steam pipes that would burn him as the train traveled along. Thankfully, his luck had changed and the pipes were cool to the touch. Oliver reached back and wedged his bag between his back and the underside of the train car, then mentally prepared for the long trip ahead.

* * * *

Oliver rode wedged on his beam, about three feet above the tracks, from Chicago into Ohio where the train made a stop in Cleveland. He welcomed the chance to relax his grip and wiggle around a bit – something he didn't dare do while the train was moving at speeds up to fifty miles an hour. Oliver didn't know it, but the brakemen were making their rounds as they oiled the bearings.

"Hey, get out from under there!" the brakeman yelled in anger when he spotted Oliver in his hiding place.

Not wanting to be hauled off to jail, Oliver squirmed off his beam and out from under the train on the opposite side from the brakeman. He ran as fast as he could and quickly lost himself in a crowd of people. When the train's whistle announced its departure from the Cleveland Station, Oliver ran around to the other side and climbed back onto his perch, unseen.

As the passenger train rolled through western Pennsylvania, its stowaway rider tried hard to fight off the urge to fall asleep. Oliver was growing very tired, and twice so far he had almost lost his balance. Each time, the thought of nearly dying right there on the tracks was enough to keep him alert for another couple of hours. Finally, when he thought he could hold on no longer, Oliver heard the long-awaited sound of the train's whistle, announcing its arrival in New York City. Loosening his grip, Oliver breathed a sigh of relief.

Jack London riding the rails… just as Oliver did

"I made it," he whispered, as tears of happiness fell silently onto the beam.

CHAPTER TWENTY

Reunited at Last

"How much for a ride to Dobbs Ferry?" Oliver asked as he peered his head into the window of the red and green paneled taxi cab. "Fifty cents per mile," the driver replied with a smirk. "No doubt more than you can afford."

Gas powered taxis were new to the city and something Oliver had never encountered during his years in Kansas. He had no idea what the fare would cost but figured there was no harm in asking. He quickly decided to stick to one of the horse-drawn carriages which were lined up at the train station, for a fraction of the cost. First, of course, he would need to have some money.

Walking around the New York City Station, Oliver found a public restroom. Once inside, he huddled into a corner and unhooked the front of his overalls, folding them down to his waist. Silently, he tore at the waist of his underwear until he had worked a small hole into the seam and managed to pull out several bills.

"That should hold me for a while," Oliver thought.

He quickly repositioned his overalls, left the restroom, and headed for the carriages.

"The Children's Village in Dobbs Ferry," Oliver spoke with authority to the driver. He had learned the location of the orphanage, where he had lived as a child, from Reverend Swan during one of his yearly visits to McCammon's farm. He hadn't seen Reverend Swan in nearly three years, but he had committed the information to memory, not knowing when, or if, he would need it.

Arriving at the front of the Administration Building, Oliver thought he remembered it being much bigger. Of course, he had been just nine years old, so everything must have seemed bigger, he reasoned to himself. As he paid the driver and headed towards the building, he heard his name.

"Hello, Oliver!" a man called out. "Well look at you, nearly a grown man. Welcome back!"

Oliver took a second but then realized that this was Reverend Swan. He extended his hand.

"Grown I am," Oliver replied with a smile as he shook the agent's hand. "Grown and on my own."

"What brings you back to The Children's Village?" Reverend Swan asked curiously.

"Well, actually," Oliver began, as the two of them walked along the path leading to the boys cottages, "you're just the man I'm looking for. I'm trying to find my brother, Edward. I was told you might know where he is."

Reverend Swan measured his words carefully, not knowing just how much of the story Oliver had been told. "Well, he did come back East," the agent began, "but he's not here at the orphanage."

"Look," Oliver spoke as he stopped along the path, "I know all about William Gish and how he overworked Edward till his back was hurt and he couldn't work anymore. Then he was done with him, and you brought him back here. Did you place him with another family, or what?"

"He is with a family, Oliver," Reverend Swan offered, "but I don't know where. Once I got him back here, he was out of my care. I suggest you go to the offices of the Children's Aid Society and ask them where he's living."

"Where's that office?" Oliver needed to know. "I'll have to get another carriage taxi."

"No need for that. I'll take you there myself," Reverend Swan offered as he waved Oliver in the direction of his car.

* * * *

Seated across a large desk from the director of the Children's Aid Society with Reverend Swan in the chair next to him, Oliver felt nearly giddy at the prospect of being so close to finding Edward.

"Well now, let's see here," the director, Robert Brace, began as he searched through the pages of a large roster book, "the year 1911... yes, here it is. 'Edward Nordmark returned to The Children's Village for training'."

As the director read from the large book, Oliver squirmed in his chair, anxious to hear more.

"Placed January of 1912 with Mr. and Mrs. James Colgrove of Tioga, New York. Here's the street address," the director said as he jotted the information down on a piece of paper and handed it to Oliver.

Looking down at the answer he now held in his hand, Oliver felt like he had just won a great prize. Did he dare ask for more?

"What about my sister, Anna? Do you have anything in there about where she is?" Oliver asked courageously. "We were separated in 1907. Could you check that year?"

Robert Brace looked at Oliver over the rim of his eyeglasses. He realized that the young man before him was searching for any connection to whatever family he may have left. He admired his tenacity.

"Well, now that would be in a different book," the director said as he rose from his seat and walked to a stack of books near the window. "Let's see... 1907... that would be... yes, here it is. It should be in this roster book."

Oliver held his breath. It had only just occurred to him to ask about Anna. Would he really be so lucky today as to learn about both his brother and his sister?

"Here it is," the director's voice broke the silence as he read from the book. "Anna Nordmark – assigned to the Sisters of Charity Orphanage in the Bronx section of New York City. There's no notation of a move from that orphanage so I would presume that she is still there. I'll give you that address as well."

Oliver did his best to maintain his composure as he took the second piece of paper from Mr. Brace. As he stood to leave, he shook the man's hand vigorously.

"Thank you kindly, sir," Oliver said, as he felt his face flush with warmth. "Thank you, thank you!"

Oliver and Reverend Swan left the office and returned to The Children's Village. Oliver stayed overnight, at the suggestion of Reverend Swan, to get a fresh start on his trip the following morning.

With enough money removed from the seam of his underwear to purchase a ticket to Tioga, and a bit more for meals, Oliver boarded the train the next day. He waved good-bye to Reverend Swan.

"Thanks for all your help," Oliver called out from his window.

"Good luck and God's speed, Oliver," the agent called back. "I hope what you find is what you're looking for!"

As the train pulled off, headed to central New York, Oliver was left to think about what Reverend Swan had meant by his parting remark.

* * * *

Standing momentarily outside the home of James Colgrove, Oliver's memories of his journey to this place raced through his thoughts. A long six years had passed since he had laid eyes on his brother. Edward was just seven years old the last time the two of them were together. Quickly, Oliver added in his head and realized that Edward was now thirteen.

"Well," he said to himself, "like our father used to say, 'nothing ventured, nothing gained' – here goes." He reached up and knocked on the door.

"Can I help you?" a kindly looking woman asked.

"Yes, I believe you can, ma'am," began a nervous Oliver. "My name's Oliver Nordmark and I've been told that my brother, Edward, lives here."

"Why yes," a surprised Mrs. Colgrove replied. "Come, in, come in."

Oliver entered the front door of the small frame house and took a quick glance around. This was a modest home with neat rooms and simple furnishings. Mrs. Colgrove motioned Oliver to the sofa in the front room.

"You just have a seat here, Oliver," she spoke as she looked Oliver over. "I'll go and fetch Edward."

Several minutes passed as Oliver sat excitedly on the sofa. Finally, he heard footsteps in the hall and then he saw him. Edward stood tall and thin with his hair clipped close to his head. The brothers stood and gazed upon each other for a long moment. Moving towards Edward, Oliver broke the silence.

"Edward," he began hesitantly, as he stepped closer, "it's me, Oliver."

The brothers reached for one another as they embraced, and the years seemed to just melt away.

"Sit down, sit down," Edward said through his smile, revealing the dimples of his childhood. "I can't believe you're really here!"

Mrs. Colgrove quietly left the room to give the brothers some private time to become reacquainted.

"I was sorry to learn from McCammon that old farmer Gish turned out to be no good. I didn't know they had sent you back East until just last week," Oliver began to explain to Edward. "Soon as I was told, I headed out of Kansas to find you."

"Where you been all this time?" Edward wanted to know.

"Well," Oliver took a deep breath, "I was at McCammon's till I was nearly fifteen. That's when I couldn't take it no more. I was doin' all the work on that farm and gettin' paid nothin'. I figured I could do as much for myself, if you know what I mean. So, I hopped a freight train out of town and ended up in Goodland, almost to the Colorado line. I worked for a couple of brothers for two years, saving up my money. After that, I went back to Esbon to try and find out where you were. That's when McCammon told me about Gish.

"What kind of work did you do?" Edward asked with curiosity.

"Well, I learned how to harvest wheat, and would you believe I learned how to build a house out of the earth? It's called a sod house," Oliver said with pride, "and before I left, I was workin' on building a frame house."

Edward and Oliver sat quietly as each of them considered all they had been through and how their lives had taken such different paths. Finally, Edward broke the silence.

"Did you come to take me away from here?" Edward asked with hopeful eyes.

Oliver was surprised by Edward's question and took a moment to reply. "Don't you like it here?" he wondered aloud. "Looks like a decent place, and Mrs. Colgrove seems real nice."

"Oh, she puts on a good show. Her and Mr. Colgrove act like they're the pillars of society, if you know what I mean," Edward spoke softly so as not to be overheard. "But soon as no one's lookin', they're mean as all get out. I don't know how much longer I can stand livin' here, I can tell you that."

Edward stood and walked slowly to the doorway, checking that Mrs. Colgrove was out of earshot. Oliver noticed right away that Edward walked with a slight limp – a result of his injuries at the Gish farm, Oliver reasoned.

"What do they do that's so mean?" Oliver questioned.

"Oh, all kinds of things. I could take a week tellin' you stories." Edward shook his head just thinking about it. "One time when I was out back workin' on my old bicycle, I got my fingers stuck in the chain. It hurt so bad, I was yellin' and screamin' for help but nobody came. I knew they were both in the house, too. I passed out a couple times, the pain was so bad, before old Mr. Colgrove finally got up to come out and see what the trouble was. He went and got a tool to cut the chain, but not before he yelled at me for bein' so stupid. I nearly lost these two fingers. You can see the deep scars, right there."

Oliver leaned over and looked at Edward's misshapen and scarred fingers. His heart felt heavy for his brother, who had suffered so badly at the hands of people who were supposed to take care of him. But what could Oliver do?

"I don't know what I can do," Oliver said sadly. "I don't have a job or a place to live myself. Besides, you're just thirteen. If I tried to take you from these people the law would probably be after us both."

"Well," a resigned Edward said as he shrugged his shoulders, "then the law's gonna have to be after just one of us, cuz I'm not stayin' here."

"Don't do that," a worried Oliver pleaded. "Just a few more years and you can leave without any trouble. I don't want you to end up in jail, Edward. Please say you'll hang in here just a bit longer."

"I'll try," Edward said, "but I ain't makin' any promises."

* * * *

At Mrs. Colgrove's insistence, Oliver stayed two nights at the little home on Maple Street, sleeping on the floor of Edward's bedroom. The brothers spent more time catching up on their missing years and talked a lot about their plans. On the morning of the third day, Oliver packed his small bag to go, as Edward watched in silence.

"I'm going to come back, Edward," Oliver promised. "I need to find work and a place of my own, then when you're old enough, you can come and live with me."

"I want to believe that," Edward said sadly.

"Here..." Oliver said as he reached into his pants pocket and brought out his watch, "here's my watch. Take good care of it till I come back... and I will be back for it."

Edward took the pocket watch and curled his fingers tightly around it. He looked up at his big brother with moist eyes.

"I'll see you soon." Oliver extended his hand to Edward. The brothers shook hands, then embraced for the final time.

"I love you, Edward," Oliver whispered as he turned and walked from the house.

CHAPTER TWENTY-ONE
Edward's Mistake

Oliver's next destination, after leaving Tioga, was back to New York City. He went to The Sisters of Charity Orphanage on Kingsbridge Road in the Bronx section. There he did indeed find his sister, Anna, who had lived with the Catholic Sisters since 1907. They sat and talked for several hours in the living room of the orphanage, getting reacquainted. To Oliver, it seemed that Anna was getting along just fine, and she seemed to be happy enough.

After several failed attempts to find work in the city, Oliver was approached by a Navy recruiting officer in his temporary home at the Salvation Army Shelter. The recruiting officer offered Oliver four years of food and shelter, along with a paycheck, for his service aboard the USS Melville, a destroyer in the Atlantic Fleet.

"Are you eighteen?" the recruiter asked. "If not, you'll need to have your guardian sign up for you."

"Well, I'm not eighteen yet, and I've got no guardian," Oliver explained. "I'm on my own you see, so I don't suppose I can sign up."

The recruiter looked around the room and nodded in the direction of the clerk seated at the front desk.

"How about that fellow at the desk over there?" the recruiter suggested. "He's old enough to sign for you. No one will know he's not your real guardian."

Always after an adventure, Oliver took just a few seconds to think it through, then signed on the dotted line. The clerk was more than happy to sign for Oliver's enlistment. With Oliver in the Navy's care, there would be one more available bed at the shelter.

* * * *

After Oliver's departure, Edward spent the next two weeks sulking around the Colgrove's house becoming more and more restless about his situation.

"Oliver was fourteen, nearly the same age as me, when he hopped that freight train out of Esbon," he reasoned to himself. "I don't see why I have to wait any longer to get away from these people."

The main problem with leaving, as far as Edward could see, was that he didn't have any money, and he had no experience hopping onto trains. Besides, with his back injury, he didn't think he would even be capable of jumping onto a train. He spent days thinking of how he could get a hold of some money to make his break. That Saturday, he saw his chance.

"Edward!" James Colgrove called up the stairs. "We're leaving to go visit Mrs. Colgrove's sister for the day. We'll be back around nightfall. I want you to get the grass cut while we're gone, and while you're at it, pull some of those weeds growing by the back fence."

"Yeah, alright," Edward called back from his room.

After the Colgroves were gone, Edward crept around the house looking into every closet, cabinet, box and niche for anything of value. The Colgroves were not a wealthy couple by any means, but they were not destitute either. Finally, under James Colgrove's bed, Edward found what he was looking for.

"Now that's a nice shotgun," he whispered aloud, as he slid the weapon out and placed it on top of the bed. "That ought to be worth somethin'."

Edward carried the gun to his room. He packed a small bag with a few things that he figured he would need to get by. As he looked around his room, his eyes caught the shiny silver of Oliver's pocket watch. Edward snatched it up and slid it into his pants pocket.

"Sorry, Oliver," he said out loud. "I can't wait any longer."

With his bag slung over his shoulder and the shotgun tucked under his arm, Edward left the house on Maple Street and never looked back.

* * * *

"No, I don't give cash for guns," the pawn shop owner informed thirteen-year-old Edward, "but I can make a trade for another gun. That's the best I can offer you."

Looking nervously around the shop, Edward tried hard to decide what to do. As he glanced past the owner's head to the back wall, he saw a row of revolvers displayed. He quickly decided that a revolver would be easier to walk around with than a shotgun.

"Alright then," Edward said with as much authority as he could muster. "I'll trade it for a revolver. One of them back there'll do just fine."

The pawn shop owner took a revolver down from the wall and showed it to Edward. He demonstrated how to load the gun, which bullets to buy, and how to clean the chamber. Edward was too nervous to remember a thing the man said.

"Is it an even trade then?" asked Edward, wanting to get out of there.

"I'll just need your name on this form and then yes, it's an even trade," the owner said as he placed a pencil and paper in front of Edward. "I'll even throw in a few bullets."

Thinking fast, Edward penciled a name on the line provided and pushed the paper back towards the shop owner.

"Lloyd Mickle," the owner read from the paper. "Well, nice doin' business with you Lloyd. That's a fair trade. Now try and stay out of trouble with it."

Edward nodded in the man's direction, picked up the revolver and quickly exited the pawn shop.

* * * *

With the revolver tucked inside his pants and covered up by his jacket, Edward nervously walked around trying to figure out what to do next. His original plan was to sell the shotgun to get enough money for a train ticket to New York City, but that hadn't worked out. He still had no money, but he did have the revolver. As he walked away from the center of town, he saw an older, well-dressed man sitting on a wooden bench. The man appeared to be alone, so without thinking of the consequences, Edward put an ill-conceived plan into motion. Casually, he walked up to the man and spoke.

"Hey, mister," Edward began. "I'm a bit down on my luck. You got any money you could spare me?"

"Get out of here, you hobo," the man said with disgust. "Get a job."

"This is my job," a shaking Edward said through gritted teeth as he jammed the barrel of his revolver into the man's side. "Now give me your money."

The man's attitude towards Edward was quickly replaced by alarm and fear. He reached into his pockets and handed over his money, sweat pouring from his brow. Edward grabbed the money and took off running.

"Help! Help! I've just been robbed!" the old man called out as he frantically waved his arms in all directions.

Three men, who had been standing a short distance away, heard the old man's shouting and took off after Edward. Running as fast as he could, Edward looked several times over his shoulder and realized that the men were closing in on him. As they caught up, the three pursuers pounced on Edward, tackling him to the ground. They wrestled his hands behind his back and hauled him back to town, delivering him directly to the sheriff's station.

Elmira Reformatory – 1911

After a brief trial the following morning, Edward stood before the judge who spoke harshly to the young offender.

"Edward Nordmark, you have committed a serious crime," the judge began, as he looked directly at Edward over the top of his eyeglasses. "However, due to your young age and lack of any prior criminal record, I consider you a candidate for rehabilitation. Therefore, I sentence you to a five year indeterminate sentence at the Elmira Reformatory. Do you have any questions?"

"Indeterminate, sir?" a nervous and shuffling Edward asked.

"Yes young man, indeterminate," the judge responded. "That means that your behavior and speed of rehabilitation will determine the length of your sentence. You will be required to attend classes to complete your education, as well as perform labor in one of the Reformatory's Work Shops. When your sentence has been completed, you will be followed by a parole officer of the state for a period of no less than two years."

The judge brought his large gavel down with a bang, then stood to leave the room. As he lowered his head, Edward was led out by a jailhouse guard to begin his rehabilitation.

CHAPTER TWENTY-TWO

Estella May

While stationed on the USS Melville, Oliver decided to write to Edward to see how he was getting along. He was surprised when the letter was returned, two months later, with a handwritten message on the envelope.

No longer at this address. Sentenced to the Elmira Reformatory for five years after committing armed robbery.

Oliver was saddened by the news. What had gone so wrong that Edward would resort to armed robbery? Did he run away and find himself without money for food or shelter? Oliver couldn't make sense of it, no matter how hard he tried. Whenever Oliver had been without money to eat, he would go to the back door of a restaurant and ask for some stale buns or bread – or a job for Heaven's sake. Never would he have reached for his gun to rob an innocent person. Where did Edward get himself a gun, anyway? The situation weighed heavily on Oliver's mind but there was nothing he could do about it while he was out to sea.

When he was issued his first leave papers, Oliver knew just what he would do. He went to the train station and purchased a ticket to Elmira, New York.

As he boarded the train and made his way down the aisle looking for a seat, he caught a glimpse of a young girl smiling up at him. He passed the girl, who was seated next to a woman that he figured must be her mother, and sat two seats back on the opposite side of the aisle. The train pulled slowly out of the station, and Oliver settled in for the long ride. Before long, the young girl stood up and walked towards Oliver.

"Can I sit with you?" she asked as she stopped at Oliver's seat.

"I don't care," Oliver responded as he wondered what was wrong with the seat she had been in. "Suit yourself."

"My name's Estella," the young girl offered. "Estella May Rarick."

Oliver glanced over at this skinny little girl, not wanting anything to do with her. He wasn't used to being around girls, but he knew he shouldn't be rude.

"Oliver Nordmark," he finally answered, then looked out the window.

"Would you like to see my magazine?" Estella asked in her sweetest voice. She offered her magazine to Oliver in an effort to engage him in conversation.

Oliver took the magazine, thumbed through its pages, but didn't have anything to say about it. He handed it back to Estella.

"My mother and I are going home to Elmira," Estella tried again. "We've been to visit my aunt in Stroudsburg, Pennsylvania. Where are you getting off?"

"Oh, I'm going to Elmira too," Oliver said as he looked back towards the young girl. "I got family there."

Estella May Rarick in Washington State – Age 14

"That sure is a nice uniform you're wearing," Estella complimented the young sailor. "Are you in the Navy?"

"Yes I am," Oliver said proudly. "I've got two more years at sea."

Estella and Oliver proceeded to get acquainted during the train ride to Elmira. Oliver learned that Estella had worked in a logging camp in Washington State, and he shared with her stories of his earlier days in Kansas. When the conductor announced that the train would be pulling into the station in fifteen minutes, Estella got up her nerve to ask Oliver what she really wanted to know.

"If I give you my address, will you write to me when you're out to sea?" she asked hopefully, holding her breath.

"Go ahead," Oliver answered with a smile, "write it down and I'll send you a letter."

Estella went back to her mother's seat and returned with a pencil. She tore a page from her magazine and jotted her address down, then handed it to Oliver. He folded the paper and slipped it into his pocket.

As the train pulled to a stop in the Elmira Station, Estella stood up and gathered her things to leave.

"Good-bye Oliver," she said with a grin, "I'll be looking for your letter."

"Good-bye Estella," Oliver replied with a half grin of his own.

* * * *

Oliver sat in the Visitor Waiting Room of the Elmira Reformatory wondering just how this visit with Edward was going to go. He rose from his seat as the door opened, and his brother was escorted into the room. The door shut behind him as Edward lowered his head.

"Edward, what happened?" Oliver broke the silence as he motioned Edward to sit. "I thought we agreed that you would stay with the Colgroves until you were older and I had a place where you could live?"

"I couldn't wait," Edward spoke softly. "I ran off with Mr. Colgrove's shotgun and traded it in at the pawn shop for a revolver. Then, I don't know what came over me, but I tried to beg money from some old guy. When he refused and called me a hobo, I just kinda snapped. I took the gun and demanded money from him. I don't know why I did it, I was desperate."

Oliver decided to change the subject. There was no use trying to go back and change anything that had already happened. They'd have to make the best of the situation now.

"So how ya gettin' along?" Oliver asked, trying to sound upbeat. "What's this place like?"

"It's okay," answered Edward, shrugging his shoulders, "beats living at the Colgroves, to tell the truth. I go to classes and I go to work. I eat and sleep, you know, the regular stuff, and I do a lot of reading."

"What kind of work do you do?" Oliver asked.

"Well, they got what they call the Piece/Price System of work here. I put together belts and suspenders, hammerin' the buckles on and drillin' the holes in the leather." Edward started to become a bit more animated as he spoke about his work. "I make three cents for every completed belt. It's a bit of money, which I never had, and it fills part of the day. It ain't bad."

Oliver and Edward spent about half an hour catching up on one another's lives until the door opened and the guard informed the brothers that their visit was over.

"I'll be out of the Navy in just two years," Oliver said in parting. "I'll be back as soon as I'm discharged."

"I'll be lookin' for you," Edward smiled as he turned to go. "Don't worry about me, Oliver. I'll be fine here."

* * * *

Back on the USS Melville, Oliver wrote a simple letter to the young girl he had met on the train.

"Why not?" he figured. "Nothin' ventured, nothin' gained. I got nothin' to lose and she seemed like a nice enough girl."

He was surprised at how quickly Estella wrote back to him. Her letter arrived with an invitation to spend Thanksgiving with her and her family. Oliver knew that he would be back at the Philadelphia Port in time for the holiday, so with no other plans, he wrote back accepting the invitation.

The train ride to Elmira was packed with holiday travelers. Oliver arrived at midday and quickly found a taxi to take him to the address that Estella had given him. He paid the driver and approached the front door with a bit of apprehension. Was this really a good idea, he wondered? He barely knew this young girl.

"Well, I'm here now," thought Oliver, as he reached up and knocked on the door.

* * * *

Oliver need not have worried. Estella introduced him to her mother, Emma Rarick, and explained that her father had passed away when Estella was just five years old. She had seven brothers and sisters, he learned, and three of them were home for Thanksgiving. Mary Ann was the oldest of the three, with George Jr. next, and Henry just in line above Estella, who was the baby of the family.

Everyone was very welcoming, and Oliver thoroughly enjoyed his visit. He was finally getting a taste of what being part of a real family was like. He now realized just what he and Edward had missed all those years.

"How are you enjoying work in the Navy?" George Jr. asked Oliver at one point during the meal.

"It's exciting work," Oliver answered. "I'm learning a lot and I'm earning a bit of money, which I'm saving for when I get out."

"That's very wise of you," Estella's brother cautioned. "You never can be too careful where money's concerned."

Oliver knew that all too well. He could get by with very little, but if he wanted to get ahead in the world, he needed to save what he could.

Estella showed Oliver around town after the Thanksgiving meal, and the two young people continued to get better acquainted. When they parted company, Oliver had decided that he liked Estella very much and would continue to write to her while he was at sea. He didn't know where the friendship might lead, but he decided to give it a shot.

* * * *

After a two year correspondence, Oliver felt that he and Estella had gotten very close. Two months before his discharge from the Navy, he wrote his final letter from the ship.

Dear Estella,

I know this may be a bit sudden, and you might think I'm being too fast, but I was hoping that when I get back on shore, maybe you would consider getting hitched. I know you'd have to ask your mother, since you're not yet sixteen, but if she would be willing to sign for you, we could get married right away. I've got some money saved up that we could live off of until I find a job. I'll wait for your answer when I get into port on April 2nd. I'll be coming into Philadelphia and hope that you'll be able to meet me. If I don't see you there, I will catch the train to Elmira.

Yours,

Oliver

* * * *

An anxious and nervous Oliver Nordmark searched the pier as the USS Melville pulled into port. He scanned the crowd, hoping that Estella had gotten permission from her mother to meet him. Most of all, he was hoping that she would accept his proposal. That would make him the happiest sailor aboard the ship. At last, he caught a glimpse of Estella, her mother at her side. She was waving her handkerchief in his direction, and her face was flushed and smiling. Oliver took that as a good sign. When the sailors were finally permitted to disembark from the ship, Oliver kept his eyes on Estella so as not to lose sight of her in the crowd.

"Oliver!" Estella called out. "Oliver, over here!"

Oliver rushed to greet Estella and the two embraced briefly. Before Oliver could even speak, Estella answered his most pressing question.

"Yes, yes! I'm answering your letter!" she began in excitement. "Mother will sign the papers and we can get married right away!"

Oliver's face filled with happiness – more happiness than he had felt in all his life.

"Thank you," he said as he shook Emma Rarick's hand a bit too hard. "You won't be sorry. I'll take good care of her. I've got some money saved up and I'm a hard worker, so I know I can get a job pretty quick."

"I'm sure everything will be just fine." Emma Rarick smiled back at the happy young man before her. "We'll make the plans as soon as we get back to Elmira."

The three travelers made their way through the crowd to the train station and waited for the boarding call to Elmira, ready to begin a new life.

"Well," Oliver said to himself proudly, "nothin' ventured, nothin' gained is certainly working out well for me!"

* * * *

Oliver Nordmark and Estella May Rarick were married in a small frame chapel in Painted Post, New York, on May 10, 1919.

The bride wore a simple white dress with a small floral print and belted waist. The groom wore a clean white shirt adorned with a thin black tie. The service was performed by the local minister, Reverend John Knox. Estella's mother, along with Reverend Knox's wife, Eunice, stood as witnesses for the young couple. They received two wedding gifts – a comb and brush set from Estella's best friend, Helen Gamble, and a cup and saucer set from Estella's mother.

As Oliver and Estella stepped out of the chapel for the first time as man and wife, Oliver took a deep breath. He didn't know for sure what the future would hold, but he knew where he had been and the many life lessons he had learned. Smiling down at his new bride, he looked forward to his chance for a happily-ever-after.

EPILOGUE

Oliver and Estella Nordmark

Oliver and Estella settled first in Corning, New York, where Oliver found work at a glass works factory. After being laid off from that job, and having no success at finding another, Oliver reenlisted in the Navy where he received both a 'shipping over pay' and a salary. He sent everything he received back to Estella and their first child, May. Estella wrote Oliver several times telling him she was having a hard time making ends meet. When he returned home on a 48-hr. leave, Oliver decided to leave the Navy and head back to Kansas, where he felt certain he could find work. As soon as he got a job following the harvest, he sent for Estella and May. Their second child, Francis – or Bud, as he came to be called – was born in Kansas. When work dried up, Oliver put Estella and the children on a train back to Pennsylvania. He didn't have enough money for a ticket himself, so he resorted to riding the rails as he had done when he was younger.

The family settled in Stroudsburg, Pennsylvania, where Oliver found work and four more children were born – Oliver, Jr., Margaret, James and Benjamin.

After a tragic accident in 1930, Oliver was left to raise his large family on his own. Those years are captured in the author's second book, *Peanut Butter For Cupcakes – A True Story From the Great Depression.*

Edward Nordmark

Edward struggled with the effects of his childhood years. He never married or had children of his own. In May of 1928, at the age of twenty-seven, he again committed armed robbery, stealing $112.00. He was sentenced to twenty years at Sing Sing Correctional Facility in Ossining, New York. A subsequent conviction earned him a life sentence. In 1958, suffering from a terminal heart condition, he was released to Oliver's care. Edward died at his brother's home in Stroudsburg, Pennsylvania, on July 1, 1958.

Anna Nordmark

Anna Nordmark stayed with the Sisters of Charity until adulthood. She later married and had three children.

Oliver Nordmark

Oliver never remarried and continued to live in Stroudsburg, Pennsylvania. He worked as a silk weaver and a house builder, eventually going to school to learn the welding trade. He traveled to Pearl Harbor to work as a welder on a reconstruction project after the infamous attack in 1941. His adventurous spirit took him all over the United States, sometimes traveling with his family, often traveling on his own. Whenever he was out West, he would stop in Esbon, Kansas to visit his old friends. He stayed in touch with the McCammons, even receiving a long letter from Hettie McCammon giving him advice on how to care for his children.

Oliver was outgoing and talkative, making friends wherever he went. Most of his twenty-three grandchildren knew him well and enjoyed spending time with him. In his sixties, Oliver learned to fly an airplane, water skied on the Delaware River, learned to scuba dive in Florida, and traveled to Mexico and Ireland, where he kissed the Blarney Stone.

At the age of ninety-five, Oliver died following an accident. He was riding his bike and accidentally turned into traffic, getting hit by a small truck. Having hit his head, he was admitted to a hospital and later transferred to a nursing home where he passed away. Oliver is buried in Prospect Cemetery, in East Stroudsburg, beside his wife and brother. As of this writing, he is survived by his youngest son, Benjamin, who is eighty-nine years old.

As his granddaughter, I am honored to have the opportunity to share his story.

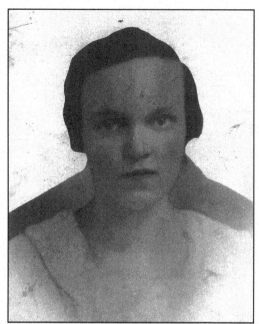

Portrait of Estella Rarick Nordmark, Circa 1925 – age 21

Oliver's Sister Anna with her daughter and grandchildren

Oliver & Estella's Children: May, Francis (Bud), Oliver, Margaret, James, Benjamin

Oliver and his Children:
Back – Oliver, Benjamin, James, Francis.
Front – May, Oliver, Margaret

Oliver in Hawaii, working on reconstruction after Pearl Harbor attack

McCammon's House in Esbon, KS – 2007

Last known photograph of Oliver, age 95,
holding great-granddaughter Estella Grace Aviles – November, 1993

Oliver, Estella, and Edward's final resting place in Prospect Cemetery, East Stroudsburg, PA

GLOSSARY

Cottonwood Poles – A type of poplar tree with cottony seeds and a strong pole like trunk.

Cow Chips – Pancake shaped, dried cow manure, baked hard by the sun, and used for fuel.

Cradle Scythe – Tool used for cutting wheat or tall grass. The blade is approximately 27" long and curved slightly upward to optimize the cut. A long handle allowed the farmer to cut without constant bending. Scythes fitted with a cradle or bow not only cut the grain, but would also scoop it up and lay it to the side in a neat path.

Crick – Variant of creek – a small, shallow stream.

Creosote – A dark, thick liquid with a pungent odor, made from coal tar and used as an antiseptic and wood preservative

Governor – Part of the mechanism on an engine that regulates the supply of fuel.

Granary – A building for storing threshed grain.

Guarish – To heal or cure.

Hayseed – A person from the country, especially a simple, unsophisticated one.

Hobo – A homeless and usually penniless wanderer. Most hobos traveled from town to town finding work when they could, but only for the sake of financing their next adventure.

Leave Papers – Signed papers given to servicemen allowing them to be away from their assigned duties for a specific period of time.

Sickle – Curved blade tool used for cutting wheat and grass in the 1800's. Working with a sickle required a lot of bending. It was back-breaking work.

Smelling Salts – A mixture of ammonia and perfume used to restore someone to consciousness by placing it under the person's nose.

Vaudeville – Traveling groups of stage entertainers popular from the 1880's – 1930's.

Willow Brush – Trees that grow along creeks and streams that have narrow leaves and strong, lightweight wood.

LESSON PLANS

<u>LEARNING OBJECTIVES</u>

- Identify key ideas of narrative non-fiction text
- Respond to literature through discussions, poetry, art, and drama
- Analyze literary elements such as plot, character, and theme
- Extend learning through multi-media activities
- Explore American history through literature

<u>DISCUSSION QUESTIONS</u>

1. Describe the housing situation for Oliver and his family when they lived at 405 E. 19th Street in New York City. How does their home compare to yours?
2. What was Oliver's punishment for playing hooky? Do you think this was a just punishment?
3. What were some of the rules the children had to follow in the orphanage? How do these rules compare to the rules your parents have set for you?
4. How did Oliver feel about being chosen to ride the Orphan Train to find a home? How would you have felt in his situation?
5. When the Orphan Train reached each town along the route west, how were the children placed with families? What could you have done to make yourself stand out and be chosen?
6. Did Oliver and Edward like the family that chose them in Bern Kansas? What was their life like on the Blauer farm?
7. On July 4, 1913, Oliver jumped on the side of a train to run away from the McCammon farm. Was this a brave thing to do? Was it foolish? Is this something you would try?
8. In his dream, Oliver goes back to a time in Esbon when he and his friends were collecting crow heads for bounty. When he insists on

burying the bodies of the dead crows, his friends thought it was a waste of time. What do you think? What does this show us about Oliver's character?

9. Before arriving in Goodland, the hobos and Oliver agree that none of them will work for less than $4.50/day plus board. When Oliver agrees to go with Burt McColl for just $4.00/day plus board, he breaks his promise to the hobos. Why did he do that? Is it ever okay to break a promise?

10. Working for John McColl, Oliver helps to build a sod house. Why were houses on the prairie made of sod? Compare sod house living to what life is like in your house.

11. When Oliver finds out that Edward is back East, he leaves Esbon to go and find him. How does he get there? Is this a journey that you could make on your own as a teenager?

12. When Oliver learns that Edward is in Tioga with the Colgroves, Reverend Swan takes him to the train station. His parting words to Oliver were, "I hope what you find is what you're looking for." What do you think he meant by that? What kind of warning might he have been trying to impart?

13. What is Oliver's reaction when he learns of Edward's criminal acts? Do you think his reaction was the right one? How else could he have reacted?

14. Having had the same start in life, and traveled west on the same Orphan Train, why do you think Oliver and Edward came to live such different lives?

15. After reading *Orphan Train To Kansas*, and the epilog of Oliver's life, give examples of how he lived by the motto, "Nothing ventured, nothing gained." What do you think of his motto? What motto would you like to live your life by?

16. When Oliver was a grown man, what do you think he had to say about the Orphan Trains?

17. The Orphan Train Movement began in 1854 and ended in 1929. For those 75 years, over 250,000 children rode the trains that took them to new homes. Do you think that the Orphan Trains were a good idea or a bad idea? Why or why not? What other solutions

might have been tried to address the problem of so many homeless, orphaned and abandoned children living on the streets of New York and other East Coast cities?

CLASSROOM ACTIVITIES AND ASSIGNMENTS

1. After reading *Orphan Train To Kansas*, test student's comprehension with a version of the game "20 Questions." Write the names of characters from the book on individual slips of paper. Divide the class into two teams. A member of one team draws a name and "becomes" that person. Members of the other team ask questions that can be answered with "yes" or "no" to discover the identity. Give teams one point for each question asked and five points for an incorrect guess. At the end of each round (set a time limit or decide how many questions can be asked), the team with the lowest score wins.

2. The Orphan Train Era began prior to the Civil War and ended on the eve of The Great Depression. Have students create a timeline from the mid-1800's through the mid-1900's showing what was going on in the country during the years that the Orphan Trains carried children throughout the nation. Some examples would include… westward migration on the Oregon Trail, the Pony Express, Presidential elections, Civil War battles, Charles Lindbergh's transatlantic flight, etc. Challenge students to add events from local, state, and world history to the time line every day. This could be an ongoing project and help students see how the pieces of history fit together.

3. Children of the Orphan Trains were not able to write letters directly to anyone without first having the letter sent to the Children's Aid Society for approval. Letters were found in CAS archives that Oliver and Edward had written to each other but had never been forwarded, thus keeping the brothers in the dark about what was happening in their lives. Imagine that you are Oliver

living on the McCammon farm and write a letter to Edward. Or, imagine that you are Edward, and write a letter to Oliver.

4. Write a poem or Haiku about Oliver and Edward or about the Orphan Train Movement.

5. Choose ten words that are relevant to *Orphan Train To Kansas* and build a word search puzzle. Trade puzzles with a classmate and try to solve.

6. With several classmates, write a short skit about a scene from the book. Ideas could include... 1. What it was like to line up on stage of the opera house... 2. Leaving school and getting lost in the blizzard... 3. Oliver's experience in the Powerhouse Jail... 4. Meeting Estella on the train to Elmira. Take turns performing your skits for the class.

7. Draw a picture to illustrate your favorite scene from the book.

8. Create a ten question, multiple choice quiz on the book. Can your classmates pass the test?

9. Create an original cover, front and back, for *Orphan Train To Kansas.*

10. On a map of the United States, locate New York City and Bern, Kansas. Draw the route between the two locations and determine the distance in miles. Oliver's trip took three days. How many miles did he travel each day? Looking at a topographic map of the United States, discuss what Oliver and Edward might have seen when looking out the train's window as they traveled through each state.

~ In part, from "Suggestions for Cross Curriculum Studies"
orphantraindepot.com

PHOTOGRAPHIC CREDITS

Joseph Petr Sod House – 1913
Fred Hultstraud History in Pictures Collection
Institute for Regional Studies and University Archives
North Dakota State University Libraries, Fargo

Main Street of Esbon, Kansas – Photographer: Ashby
Collection Name: Images of Kansas Towns and Cities
Wichita State University Libraries Dept. of Special Collections

Children's Village Cottage – Cottage "Family" Out For A Ride
Westchester County Historical Society Collection

Orphan on Steps, Company Headed West
From the archives of NY Juvenile Asylum

McCammon's House – Collection of Gail Colson

Bern Opera House – Collection of Amelia Wicki

Man Hopping Into Boxcar, Jack London Under Train – Library of
Congress

Winter in Kansas, Oliver By Tree, Portrait of Estella,

Oliver's Children in the Care of the Children's Aid Society,
Oliver and His Grown Children – Circa 1954, Gravestones, Oliver in
Hawaii – Collection of Benjamin E. Nordmark Sr.

Binding and Shocking Wheat – Oliver on Horseback – Anna Nordmark
From the collection of James B. Nordmark

Estella in Washington State Caring for a Blind Cow
From the collection of Ed Hall, son of May Nordmark Hall

ABOUT THE AUTHOR

A Delaware resident, Donna Nordmark Aviles is the eighteenth grandchild of Oliver and Estella Nordmark. As a member of the National Orphan Train Historical Society of America, as well as the Delaware Humanities, Aviles has traveled the country speaking at schools, libraries, and community organizations. She is passionate about sharing with audiences the little-known history of the Orphan Train Movement.

Orphan Train To Kansas is based on Oliver Nordmark's oral history, as recorded by the author's father, Benjamin Nordmark, Sr. The companion book, *Peanut Butter For Cupcakes: A True Story From The Great Depression*, is the continuation of Oliver's life story as he struggles to raise his six children, after the sudden loss of his young wife. That book was honored with the BRAGMedallion Award in 2012.

Both books offer a social history and personal perspective of two important periods of American history. To learn more, or to schedule an author visit, go to:

www.orphantrainbook.com